CADET TH_____ _____
★ MEMORIAL FOUNDATION ★
Inspiring and Developing Young Leaders of Character

Read Tom's Story at www.CadetTom.com.

Greater love has no one than this: to lay down one's life for one's friends. —John 15:13 (NIV)

www.GoldStarHarley.com

www.WeAreOSD.org

OSD salutes military personnel, veterans, and their families.

OSD is a global, chapter-based Veteran Support Ecosystem (EIN 27-3842517) providing relevant, relatable, and sustainable impact to the military community through social, professional, and service-oriented programs. Since 2010, OSD has impacted over seven hundred thousand members of the military community through these award-winning programs. Read more at https://weareosd.org/.

PRAISE FOR STEP OUT, STEP UP

"Step Out, Step Up: Lessons Learned from a Lifetime of Transitions and Military Service is a mouthful for a title! When I saw it, I shuddered and thought I would call Echo Garrett and advise her to abbreviate it—I was wrong. Mark Green changed my mind with his riveting story. Every single one of those words has profound significance.

"'Step,' 'Out,' 'Up,' 'Lessons,' 'Learned,' 'Lifetime,' 'Transitions,' 'Military,' 'Service.' Focus on each concept, read the book, and you will have an authentic working outline for growth and success!

"I have spent most of my life around tough guys who had difficult, often brutal backgrounds. Some fought through, beat the odds, and prospered. Many fell by the wayside, victims of the very syndromes Green describes in chilling detail. The ones who survive and thrive have three things in common: Guts, Integrity, and Empathy. It takes courage to open one's soul to the world the way Green has here. Integrity is required to own the many mistakes Green admits, and to describe in vivid detail what was done to address each one. Finally, and most importantly, if Lieutenant Colonel Mark Green is on your team, he will never let you down.

"Every great team in any pursuit has owned that prerequisite: a bunch of folks who refuse to quit on one another. This book is valuable because it is well written and fun to read. It is priceless because it points the way to that which matters most in family and team life."

—Bill Curry, NFL player
Two-Time Super Bowl Champion
SEC & ACC Football Coach of the Year

"Colonel Green's story is compelling. His experiences almost ensure his early life track would end with him on the wrong side of the justice system serving time for flaunting society. The fact he was able to completely change all of that and have a successful military career says more about his determination and dedication to change than it does about the military environment into which he plunged. His interest in the martial arts enabled him to develop a formal discipline that stood him in good stead in a very structured society.

"His book is outstanding and reads like a fictional novel where the main character suffers as a child, digs deep into his psyche, determines what he doesn't want to become, and through hard work and dedication to perfection, becomes a major success."

—Robert Sholly
US Army Colonel (Retired)
Nobel Peace Prize Laureate
Author of *Young Soldiers Amazing Warriors* and *Soul of Success*

"Five Diamonds in the Pulpwood Queen's tiara. *Step Out, Step Up* and *Warrior's Code 001* are my November Book of the Month picks for 2018."

—Kathy L. Murphy
Founder of the Pulpwood Queens and Timber Guys Book Club

"Mark Green's *Step Out, Step Up* is one of my Top 10 #READTOLEAD books for 2017. His inspiring story is life-changing and special to me."
—Lisa Sharkey
Senior Vice President and Director of Creative Development for HarperCollins

TO
JULIA,

STEP OUT, STEP UP

STAY IN
THE FIGHT !

ALSO BY MARK E. GREEN
WITH ECHO MONTGOMERY GARRETT

Warrior's Code 001

STEP OUT, STEP UP

LESSONS LEARNED FROM A LIFETIME OF TRANSITIONS AND MILITARY SERVICE

Mark E. Green

Lieutenant Colonel, United States Army (Retired)

with Echo Montgomery Garrett

BOOKLOGIX®
Alpharetta, GA

This book includes information from many personal experiences of the author. It is published for general reference with the intent of inspiring hope. The book is sold with the understanding that neither the authors nor publisher is engaged in rendering any legal, psychological, or medical advice. The authors and publisher specifically disclaim any liability, loss, or risk, directly or indirectly, for events, advice, and information presented within. If you are a military service member, veteran, or family member of a veteran or military service member and know you need assistance with your mental health, please call this twenty-four-hour number for the Veteran Crisis Line at 1-800-273-8255, or you can text a message to 838255. Another option is a crisis line that operates independently of the military or any government agency called the Military Hotline: 888-457-4838 or text MIL1 to 839863 . This hotline connects you with veterans and others familiar with the military culture.

Although the authors and publisher have prepared this manuscript with utmost care and diligence and have made every effort to ensure the accuracy and completeness of the information contained within, we assume no responsibility for errors, inaccuracies, omissions, or inconsistencies.

ATTN: QUANTITY DISCOUNTS ARE AVAILABLE TO YOUR COMPANY, EDUCATIONAL INSTITUTION, OR NONPROFIT ORGANIZATION
for reselling, educational purposes, subscription incentives, gifts, or fundraising campaigns.

ISBN: 978-1-63183-210-9

Library of Congress Control Number: 2017917118

10 9 8 7 6 5 4 3 2   0 2 0 2 1 8

Printed in the United States of America

♾This paper meets the requirements of ANSI/NISO Z39.48-1992 (Permanence of Paper)

Cover and author photos: Kevin Garrett/www.KevinGarrett.com
Cover and jacket design: Randall Paulk
All photos courtesy Mark Green unless otherwise indicated

To honor the inspiration in life I received from my great-grandfather Jesse Kent, Senior Grand Master Edward B. Sell, Grand Master Bong Yul Shin, Charles Roth, Jim Youngquist, retired Santa Clara Sheriff Bart Bacolini, retired Lieutenant General Robert Flowers, Jack Canfield, and Lisa Sharkey; and that I continue to receive from my wife, Denise, and my children, Stephanie, Amy, Scott, and Adam.

Your leadership was true.
You shared your strengths, so I could grow.
You gave me purpose and drive.
You added value to my life far beyond what
I could have imagined.

*You gain strength, courage, and confidence by every
experience in which you really stop to look fear in the face.
. . . You must do the thing you think you cannot do.*

—Eleanor Roosevelt

CONTENTS

Preface: Stay in the Fight   xi

Chapter One: Bring the Fight   1

Chapter Two: The Log Cabin   7

Chapter Three: Champions   13

Chapter Four: Chaos   23

Chapter Five: Searching   27

Chapter Six: Gypsies, Tramps, and Thieves   37

Chapter Seven: Attitude Adjustment   45

Chapter Eight: Airborne   49

Chapter Nine: Warrior Athlete   57

Chapter Ten: Breaking Through   63

Chapter Eleven: The French Connection   69

Chapter Twelve: No Fairy-Tale Ending   73

Chapter Thirteen: An Officer and a Gentleman   79

Chapter Fourteen: Third Time's the Charm   83

Chapter Fifteen: A Miracle   87

Chapter Sixteen: On the Move   93

Chapter Seventeen: Deployed   97

Chapter Eighteen: Learning to Walk Again   101

Chapter Nineteen: The Stories We Tell Ourselves   105

Conclusion: A New Mission   109

Acknowledgments   115

Index   121

STAY IN THE FIGHT

Victory is always possible for the person who refuses to stop fighting.

—Napoleon Hill

My name is Mark Green, and I am a soldier. I am a retired Lieutenant Colonel who started out as a private in the US Army. In my thirty-four years in combat boots, I have learned to stay in the fight.

Given my background, it was doubtful that I would have ever achieved many of the things I have in my life.

I lived in a family of eight and had little to nothing growing up. My family went through some extremely difficult trials. Among the eight of us, my family and I have been affected by all kinds of struggles: everything from alcoholism, physical and mental abuse, AIDS, a family member's unsolved murder, rape, a shooting, crack-cocaine addiction, thirteen divorces, suicide, problems with the law, and much more.

I had one absentee father and three stepfathers. My mother couldn't work and watch us at the same time. I didn't even graduate from high school with my classmates due to a fluke. I subsequently ended up in some trouble that forced me to step off the dangerous path I was on and step up to a new one.

My life has always been two steps forward, one step back.

Once I joined the Army in December of 1982, I never looked back. I have given thirty-four years in total, including twenty-four years of active duty, with no break in service. I served in the 82nd Airborne on active duty, the National Guard as a combat arms–enlisted soldier and as an officer, and as both a part- and a full-time

Army Reserve soldier. In Afghanistan, my assignment was as an Inspector General in charge of the southern half of the country along the red desert from the borders of Pakistan to Iran. That job requires you to be the eyes and ears of the commander on the ground.

After I came back, transition was not what I expected. Things were different. My wife, Denise, and son Adam, then eleven, were different, and I was different. I could not shake the anxious feelings I was having.

The Army had been teaching us resilience training for a while. Some of it stuck, and some of it didn't. It just did not seem to be enough.

My request for compassionate reassignment to Florida, where my mother had taken ill and was getting much worse, was refused. My wife and our teenage son relocated to Orlando from a place we loved in Mountainview, California. I was given an assignment that put me within driving distance of my mom, wife, and son—albeit a long one—but because of a denial of a compassionate reassignment, my orders only got me as far as Atlanta and Fort Gillem, Georgia.

Once again, I was separated from my family.

I was living in South Atlanta in what I called the "Hobo Hotel." Gunshots regularly rang out nearby at night, and the small apartment I'd rented wasn't remotely what was promised. It was a far cry from our home in California. I was alone and depressed over my inability to take care of my mother, while my wife had to shoulder the bulk of that duty, too. I tried to keep my dog, Mohawk, for company, but he barked during the day when I was gone, so I had to take him back to the family in Florida.

I reached a place where I was gripped with fear that my third marriage was about to fall apart. The full weight of the situation came crashing in on me.

I was at a breaking point.

I was fifty-two years old. My post-traumatic stress from my youth, coupled with the stress of the twelve-month deployment and the specter of third divorce, put me in a tailspin. I felt so alienated that it did not seem worth it to live.

I decided to take action. I buckled down and told myself I was not going to be a statistic. To take the stress off, I started rewriting a book that I'd been working on off and on over the years. I had lots of hours to myself and thought it might be cathartic to get some of my life experiences down on paper. I spent my off-hours polishing my manuscript.

At the same time, a book called *My Orange Duffel Bag: A Journey to Radical Change* that I'd been given several months before at a police convention I attended with a friend of mine who was a sheriff caught my eye. I'd never read it, but now I had plenty of time on my hands.

Soon I was engrossed in the story of a young man who, like me, had to break out of his whacked-out environment. Like me, he kept his homelessness secret from his high school and was an athlete who lived out of district. He was awarded a scholarship to play football for Georgia Tech. Despite long odds, he overcame and went on to be a successful family man and business executive.

When I looked at who wrote it, I saw the words "brought to life by Echo Garrett." Then I noticed that she lived in Metro Atlanta. Shortly after the New Year in 2015, I reached out to her on her Facebook author's page.

I was stunned when she wrote me back and asked to see my manuscript. I was even more surprised when she emailed me after reading it and told me I had a lot of good material. She took on my project, because she believed there was enough there to make a difference for others.

I asked my Staff Judge Advocate if I could have permission to work on the manuscript with someone else as long as I did not publish until the Army looked at it. He agreed.

I always pushed myself to be the best at what I did after I joined the Army. I've achieved the rank of Lieutenant Colonel, served in Afghanistan as an Inspector General, and was based in Orlando, Florida, where I qualified for a second time to serve as an Inspector General, a position I had already held once which requires me to be the conscience of the Commander in upholding the Army values by keeping the Army moving along with good order and discipline.

Military service gave me the tools to succeed. All I had to supply was the drive, determination, and dedication. I wrote this book to help others identify what it takes to have a winning spirit, to inspire and help others during the trials and challenges of transition. My intent in sharing my stories with veterans, soldiers, and their families is to help ignite positive change in their lives by encouraging them to approach challenges in a different way. I reveal the steps I've taken to become more resilient and improve my resilience in *Warrior's Code 001*.

The lessons we learn—even the painful ones—make us who we are. I hope challenged youth who find themselves in similar circumstances to what I experienced will benefit from me sharing with them that the decisions they make right now will be enduring and matter, just as mine did. Even a seemingly small decision can have a dramatic impact on your life and those around you.

It was unlikely I would ever experience such a full life and be so blessed. I believe my faith was preparing me all this time to become a warrior for hope for my military brothers and sisters and their families.

CHAPTER ONE

BRING THE FIGHT

You must concentrate upon and consecrate yourself wholly to each day, as though a fire were raging in your hair.

—Taisen Deshimaru

I size up my final opponent while I warm up for our match. The sounds of body blows being landed and kicks connecting hard echo across the crowded gym. I am competing in the taekwondo tournament to determine who will represent the state of North Carolina in the nationals.

I won my first two matches. Now only one man stands between the gold medal in lightweight black belt and me. I root for my teammate Rafael Medina, a soft-spoken Puerto Rican from Humacao, while he takes apart his final opponent in the bantamweight class.

A big smile spreads across my face as I watch him fight with such heart and skill. I can hardly believe that only two months earlier, Medina didn't even have a white belt. But then again, until this day, I haven't put on a *gei* to fight in a tournament in the four years since I was a high school senior.

Fellow enlisted man Pedro Laboy put out a call looking for team members to represent Fort Bragg, where we are assigned to the 82nd Airborne Division and 18th Airborne Corps, in the state taekwondo tournament. Medina and I, along with two others, are the only ones who showed up.

"We have no support from our CO," Laboy tells us. "All our training will have to be in our off-hours."

"What off-hours are you talking about?" I ask, laughing. Medina and Laboy crack smiles, too.

Our schedules are grueling, barely allowing time for sleep, much less training for a sport that isn't officially recognized by the US Army. We train at the Callahan Boxing Gym on Fort Bragg, the Morale, Welfare, and Recreation Center, and wherever we can find.

Then Laboy, also from Puerto Rico, shares his secret dream: "I want us to be the first team to wear the US Army colors in the national competition in Dayton, Ohio. Taekwondo has just become an Olympic sport, and we can do this."

The three of us who qualified for the state tournament make an unlikely trio.

I'm a loud, towheaded country boy from Missouri. I wheedled my way into a taekwondo class at age twelve. My little brother and I amassed a collection of 178 trophies as kids, mostly in tournaments all over the Midwest. As a junior competitor, I placed second in a national tournament. Then I also competed in Dayton, Ohio, at the nationals as a black belt after my senior year in high school. With a single mom, there was never enough money to get the training I needed to be competitive at that level. I didn't medal, but I still continued to train off and on after high school.

Laboy is the only one among us with any experience in our sport on an international stage.

Taekwondo lessons had been Laboy's present from his father on his thirteenth birthday, because he was concerned that his gentle giant of a son was being bullied. As a teen, Laboy represented Puerto Rico in the light-heavyweight division at the World Invitational Taekwondo Tournament in July 1979. After joining the military and being stationed in South Korea, he got permission to represent Puerto Rico in the heavyweight division at the Pan American Games.

Medina, who Laboy met briefly when they were both stationed in South Korea, held a black belt in *kyokushinkai* karate and fought in the bantamweight division. Laboy convinced him that he could get him ready to fight as a black belt in a new style of martial arts in just two months.

I've never seen anybody work harder than Medina. Laboy's vigorous training sessions are rooted in the Korean style of the sport and emphasize speed, agility, and flexibility. I always trained in the traditional Korean style of taekwondo, because I trained under Senior Grand Master Edward Sell of Florida, who was the highest-ranking non-Asian black belt in the world, and Grand Master Bong Yul Shin of Missouri. I am rusty, but that quickly falls away once we start training together.

Laboy patiently coaches us, but he never holds back when sparring, even though he outweighs each of us by fifty pounds or more, and he towers over Medina and me. We usually train once our duties are done for the day and everybody else is getting some shuteye.

Medina goes from a white belt to a red belt in short order. He barely blinks when Laboy tells him he only has a few days to learn eight new forms required for a black belt so that he can compete at the North Carolina state tournament, which is a qualifier for the US Taekwondo Championships.

Medina quietly goes to work. He successfully tests for his black belt and then boards a plane that afternoon for his scheduled leave in Puerto Rico.

***

So now my moment has come. The referee calls my opponent, who has a Korean instructor, and me to the center of the mat. My breathing slows, and I can feel my heartbeat in my ears. All I see is my adversary. I stand across from him, knowing whoever wins will represent the state at the nationals.

As I stand staring in his eyes, I see that he wants this as badly as I do.

He scores the first point with a perfectly placed kick to my chest, but I answer his blow with one of my own. The first round goes in my favor. The second belongs to him.

Medina has secured the gold. I know Laboy dominated his first two matches. As a heavyweight, Laboy's match will be the last of the day. He acts as my coach. When I go to my corner, he whispers in my ear, "You've got this. Now finish it. Bring the fight to him."

I see Medina standing off to the side, wearing that signature serious look with his arms crossed, watching the action intently. "We're family," he mouths to me and gives me a thumbs-up.

I love winning. But when I fought as a kid, it was just for me. I didn't feel any particular allegiance to anyone other than my coach and my brother. When I enlisted in the US Army at age twenty-one, I felt like I was a part of something important, like I belonged for the first time in my life.

And now this time—competing again at a sport that gave me a taste of discipline when I had none, a sport that gave me a safe place where honor mattered when my home life was in shambles—I feel a great responsibility.

In just two short months these two guys—who I can't even understand half the time, because they are speaking rapid-fire Spanish to each other—have become my family. We are united in our determination to represent the US Army.

Nobody from the base comes out to watch us. I don't care. The only thing I care about is making sure I don't let my brothers Medina and Laboy down.

By the third and final round, I am tired. He is tired. But something inside tells me I have not given it all I can give yet. I have a little bit left. I'm going to find it. I'm going to look for that difference between winning and losing right here, right now, right this second.

I outscore my opponent by digging in deep. I get so aggressive in the final minute that I break my toe, but my adrenaline is pumping so strongly that I don't even feel it. I keep my eyes down, waiting for the decision, but I know that I've won even before the referee holds my arm up to signify my victory. The words of Mr. Roth, my first instructor, come up in my head: "You are a champion." Relief and pure joy sweep over me. I take my pads off and let the cool air hit my skin.

Any good athlete knows that the difference between winning and losing sometimes is giving that extra little bit when you think you have nothing left to give. Life is like that. When you give a little bit more when you think you've already given all you can give, that's when the magic happens.

Mark after winning gold at the North Carolina Taekwondo State Championship
(photo credit: Pedro Laboy)

When the medals are awarded for each weight class, all three of us have the gold hanging around our necks.

"You know what this means? We're going to the nationals," says Laboy, grabbing me so hard in a bear hug that I can hardly breathe.

The local newspaper writes up our victories, and the article catches the eye of Master Myong Mayes. She writes a letter to the base commander and asks to sponsor us as an official US Army team for the nationals in Dayton, Ohio.

After we make the local news, each of our commanding officers support and congratulate us on our wins. My commanding officer says, "We're proud of you, and we want you to wear the black and gold proudly," he says. "We're behind you all the way. Let me know whatever you need."

CHAPTER TWO

THE LOG CABIN

Success is to be measured not so much by the position that one has reached in life as by the obstacles which he has overcome while trying to succeed.

—Booker T. Washington

When I start school, our parents move the entire kit and caboodle of us rambunctious kids—all six of us—from our hometown of Moberly, Missouri, to a rented log cabin deep in the Ozark countryside.

During the warmer months, I spend every waking moment outside: catching snakes and lizards; fishing for catfish and sun perch with my friends; playing on the rope swing and playing ball; and helping my mom in the garden when I'm not too busy chasing garden snakes.

Log Cabin, Fenton, Missouri

After a hard rain, one of my favorite things is searching for old Indian Head pennies around our cabin and arrowheads in the freshly plowed wheat and corn fields surrounding it. I play in the nearby creek catching frogs and catfish that get swept down during heavy rains.

I love running barefoot through the woods, building tree forts, and riding bikes with my brothers and sisters on the country roads. My favorite spot during the summer is a cold waterhole where we swim. I only come indoors when the sun falls.

When the chill of winter settles in, I make blanket forts inside with my younger twin brothers and put on layers and layers of clothes so that we can stay out and play in the snow. We make snow angels and snow forts. We wage snowball fights and slide across the ice puddles in the driveway.

Dad is gone constantly, working his insurance-sales job at New York Life or doing his duty with the National Guard one weekend a month. I practice my salute whenever he's dressed in his uniform and spend hours shining his black Army boots. My dad is my hero. I live for the rare moments when he agrees to toss the ball with me after work. Every chance I get, I listen on our transistor radio to Jack Buck, the radio announcer for the St. Louis Cardinals, call the games.

On the morning of my eighth birthday on September 17, 1970, I wake up to find a baseball bat, a glove, and a new ball next to my bed on the second floor where all of us kids sleep.

It's a sign.

I daydream about baseball all the time, and my dad knows it. I shout at the top of my lungs with pure joy. Now I know Dad will play with me whenever I ask him.

That evening Dad comes home long after Mom has washed the dinner dishes and put them away. Their voices grow louder and louder. They fight a lot, but this time sounds different. Dad's words sound funny—slow and garbled. He's drunker than usual and manhandles Mom, who looks fragile and frightened.

Everything looks like it's moving in slow motion, like that moment when the pitcher releases the ball and you hold your breath waiting to see if it's a strike.

My mom grabs the phone. Dad pauses for a moment, his green eyes bloodshot and his stocky frame unsteady as he leans against the doorframe. He glares at us kids. We are all crying. Then he turns, slamming the screen door shut behind him. I hear the crunch of the tires on our dirt-and-gravel driveway as Dad wheels his forest-green VW Bug into the night.

My sisters' muffled sobs keep me awake. I finally fall asleep with my baseball glove as my pillow. My last thought as I drift off: *I wonder when Dad will come home to play ball with me?*

But he doesn't come home the next night. Or the next. Or the one after that.

Soon after that night, our parents divorce. Dad moves into a small trailer next to the Chrysler plant in Fenton off of Interstate 44. He comes around once in a blue moon with his latest girlfriend in tow. Next time I see him, he's driving a new, red car that he keeps polished like a new penny.

I watch my mom struggle. She and Dad were still in high school when she got pregnant with my oldest sister, and she was just shy of eighteen when she and Dad had a shotgun wedding. All she's ever done during their ten-year marriage is have babies, cook and clean, and try to keep Dad coming home.

Mom, Nikki Sue Hendren Green

Now she is alone and faced with three boys and three girls to feed. As the oldest boy—my twin brothers are just four years old when Dad chooses drinking and chasing women over us—I feel protective of her. But there isn't much I can do, except be near her when she cries while sorting through the ever-growing pile of bills on our kitchen table. While she smokes her Tareyton 100's, I hover behind her and pat her back and say, "It's going to be okay, Mama."

But nothing is okay anymore. I hear her on the phone sometimes, begging Dad to send a few dollars to support us. The calls usually end abruptly with Mom's red-rimmed eyes leaking tears. She'll check the mailbox religiously for a while, but his promises are as empty as the beer cans that littered our house when he was here.

Mom gets a job at United Van Lines as a receptionist. I notice that she dresses carefully for work, putting on a slash of red lipstick that emphasizes her white skin and long, dark hair. A five-foot-two ringer for Loretta Lynn and a coal miner's daughter herself, Mom tells us proudly that she is the only woman at the office. Soon she's gone all the time, either working or going on dates.

I can always tell when she's fixing up for what she hopes is a special date. She hums around the house, her smile bright and hopeful as she dabs on extra perfume.

"I'll be back soon," she calls cheerily as the door slams behind her. "You kids be good."

***

With Mom hardly ever around and Dad MIA, we kids get wilder and wilder. We run through the house and fight over what to watch on the TV. The girls want to watch *The Brady Bunch* while we boys want to watch an Army show called *Combat*.

I go from being a happy-go-lucky kid whose biggest challenge was digging enough worms for all the fishing I had planned for the day to worrying about whether there'll be any food for dinner that night. We don't eat like other families eat. We eat whatever food stamps will buy. Breakfast and dinner are often cinnamon toast. Mom rarely cooks anymore.

I am angry all the time. All of my friends have fathers. Nobody else I know has a dad who is MIA.

I have always been the fastest boy in my class at school. I'd burn off energy chasing the girls on the playground. Now I take out my frustration by constantly getting in scraps with other boys. My dad—a mix of Irish, English, and Finnish—had done some boxing, so I suppose I am trying to imitate a piece of him.

My second-grade teacher is one of the only people in my life who takes notice of me at all. She talks sweetly to me and has fish in her classroom and sometimes treats us to hand-cranked, homemade ice cream. I hate school, but I like Miss Hendricks. She's pretty, and she smells nice. She acts like she somehow sees only the good boy that I want to be.

By my fourth-grade year, my reputation and my temper keep me in trouble constantly. I spend most of my time in the hallway getting paddled. Miss Hendricks, with her soft words and tender voice, seems like someone I created in my imagination. Now teachers refer to us as "those Green kids," and I know they don't mean anything good.

CHAPTER THREE

CHAMPIONS

I have heard it said that the first ingredient of success—the earliest spark in the dreaming youth—is this: dream a great dream.

—John Alan Appleman

When I turn eleven, Mom's efforts to find us a new father finally pay off. Mom marries Mr. Robert Ferguson, a widower from Fenton with three boys—Bobby, Gary, and Richie—and a girl named Jo Ann. He moves himself and his children into our log cabin. A tall man who slicks his dark hair back, Mr. Ferguson, as he instructs us to call him, never smiles. Hugs are out of the question.

I quickly learn that Mr. Ferguson, a teamster who works at a furniture store, fancies disciplining his kids with a belt for the smallest of infractions. Any time he gets mad at Mom, he takes his anger out on his own kids. His oldest son, quiet and introverted, usually catches the brunt of it.

After dinner sometimes, he entertains himself by shooting stray cats with his .30-06 rifle. "In the morning before school, I want you to bury that damn cat," he tells us boys.

One morning his dark-green Impala won't start. He stands staring at it for a minute, smoking his cigarette down to the nub. Then he grabs gasoline for the lawnmower, dumps it all over his car, and then lights another cigarette. He flicks the match onto his own car, setting it on fire. He nonchalantly walks back into the house and calls the fire department, so he can file an insurance claim. From our boys' bedroom upstairs, I watch through the wood-pane window when the firemen come and put it out.

This is nothing like *The Brady Bunch* the girls always want to watch. After a year with all twelve of us living in the cabin, Mr. Ferguson announces that we are moving to a house that he owns in town.

I am desperate at the thought of leaving the only happy place I've ever known. The thought of trading the freedom of bare feet all summer long and no curfew because Mom knows we're fine playing outside suffocates me. *Maybe I should run away and just hang out here in the woods. But then who would stick up for my brothers and sisters? Besides, winter is coming.* My thoughts are racing, and I feel stuck.

Mr. Ferguson's house only has three bedrooms, so the three girls share two rooms upstairs while my mother and stepdad take the master bedroom. All six of us boys live in the dank, cold, unfinished basement with no privacy or walls. The laundry for twelve people is always piled in a mildew-smelling mountain mess on the floor. The noise from clothes being thrown down the chute is a constant. Worst of all, we are sleeping right under the newlyweds' bedroom. I hate him for that.

***

I notice the Teamsters' emblem, which has two horse heads, prominently displayed all over his house. Mr. Ferguson builds out the garage like a family room. It has indoor/outdoor carpet and a small color console television that gets three channels when the aluminum foil–wrapped antenna is turned just right. The poor reception frequently causes him to let loose a string of cuss words.

Up until I turn twelve, I am a frequent target for his belt. He always finds one of his bazillion rules that he accuses me of breaking. That changes one day when he decides that it's time for me to take yet another whipping.

My mom is standing in the kitchen with us, and he instructs me to go into the bedroom.

"Nope, I am done with you hitting me with your belt," I respond, holding his weird, glittery, dead fish–eyed gaze.

He looks at my mom to get her to force me to obey. She stares back at him for a moment, then shrugs her shoulders and turns away and keeps doing the dishes.

That day the beatings end.

Mr. Ferguson puts what little food is in the house under lock-and-key at night. Our two families fight constantly. I especially don't get along with the oldest boy, Bobby. He's a ghost of a kid — pale and quiet, always slipping around the house silently. We have nothing in common, except that I suspect he hates his dad almost as much as I do, especially since he's his dad's favorite target for the belt.

The house becomes a war zone.

The end comes after almost a year under his roof. He and Mom fight all through the night until she has to leave in the wee hours for her early-morning shift at the donut shop. She calls us from work to warn us to stay out of his way.

I herd my brothers and sisters into the family room to watch TV. As soon as he gets home from work, Mr. Ferguson stalks in. He snatches the TV cord out of the wall, takes it in his hands, and breaks it in half.

"This is my TV," he snarls and walks out.

"Let's all go downstairs and sit on my bed until Mom comes home," I whisper to my brothers and sisters. We pile on my makeshift pallet on the floor and sit in the uncomfortable silence of a horror movie right before the bad guy pops out of the closet.

Then we hear his footsteps on the stairs. I ball up my fists. Ready.

He never says a word. He walks around and unscrews every lightbulb in the basement and leaves us huddled together, shivering in the dark.

Now what do I do? I think. After several minutes, I tell everybody to hold hands, and I lead all my brothers and sisters upstairs through the darkness and quietly out the front door. We huddle up like a bunch of puppies on a cold night on the sewer lip, waiting for Mom to get home from her job at the donut shop.

When she sees us sitting outside, she throws her car in park and jumps out. Mom's brow knits tightly together, and she purses her lips. She doesn't ask anything, because she knows what happened.

Mom straightens her shoulders, pulls herself up to her full height of five-foot-two, and goes inside. We hear shouting, and we watch through the living-room picture window as she hurls a cup at Mr. Ferguson and then marches out the front door.

Mr. Ferguson calls the police on Mom. He has a cut above his eye.

The police arrive and manage to calm Mom, who is madder than a wet hen, down a notch and then they leave.

"Get your things," she says to us. "You have ten minutes to pack up. We're leaving."

***

She takes us two hours away to Grandpa and Grandma's small place in Moberly. When they saw the red dirt cloud trailing Mom's old beater as she drove up the driveway, they came out on the front porch to welcome us. Even though they both stand about five feet and nothing, they loom large in my life. Grandma rubs her hands—covered in flour from prepping her famous fried chicken—on one of her ever-present aprons. She is a good country cook, and my mouth starts watering, knowing that there's probably green beans, biscuits, and my favorite, red Jell-O fruit cocktail, already laid out for us along with the crispy fried chicken.

Sure enough, I'm right. She keeps a full pitcher of Kool-Aid chilling in the fridge, too. I ask for seconds on the Jell-O. Grandma's already got the card table set up for us kids to eat at so that Mom, Grandpa, and she can talk privately at the small kitchen table.

I strain to hear what they are saying. *I wonder how long we'll get to stay?* Their house seems like heaven to me after where we've been.

Since retiring from the coal mine, Grandpa keeps a used car lot at the back of their ten acres. I love to explore the old cars back there. He keeps bikes for all of us stored under the house so we can ride the dusty dirt roads surrounding their place whenever we come to visit. His catfish pond makes for good fishing, and sometimes after we clean the fish, Grandma will fry up what we catch.

In the evenings after dessert, and Grandma chasing us out of the kitchen for the umpteenth time, we crowd into the spare bedroom and play board games like Sorry!® or Operation®. On nice nights, we sit out on the porch swing and listen to the crickets.

I don't mind taking baths at Grandma's house, because she has a special soap that floats in the tub. It's called Ivory® and smells good.

Mark with his catch after a day of fishing at Grandpa Jesse Kent's

People joke about my grandpa driving his big red Buick down the dusty Missouri road to his house, saying that they can tell it's Bill from a country mile. You cannot see anyone driving that car. All you see is this big cloud of dust as he whirls by.

That Christmas, Grandma makes the season extra special by putting out treats for us like orange slices, nuts, and homemade fudge.

We've lived with them a little more than a month when I freeze—not from the cold, but from the sight of Mr. Ferguson driving up the driveway one afternoon. Mom doesn't come out of the trailer to talk to him. She doesn't get the chance even if she wants to. Mr. Ferguson has no more than put one foot on the porch when Grandpa jerks his double-barrel shotgun off the rack on the wall and flies out the door. I've never seen my grandpa move so fast.

"Get off of my porch, you S-O-B, and no, you can't speak to my daughter," he yells with the shotgun pointed squarely at Mr. Ferguson's heart. "She is never coming back to a lowdown scumbag like you."

Without a word, Mr. Ferguson turns on his heels.

After a few months, my mom borrows $5,000 from my grandpa to buy a trailer home in High Ridge in Jefferson County. She is proud to finally have a place of her own. It has three bedrooms and one and a half bathrooms.

It also has a leaky roof and is poorly insulated. The toilets clog and sometimes you get a shock when you use it due to the poor quality of the aluminum wiring. The hot-water heater is not big enough to produce enough hot water for a family of seven. Just think what it is like to have only one washer and dryer and six children's dirty clothes piling up.

The rain beats down on the metal roof and keeps me awake at night. The windows leak, forming sweat due to their poor quality and making water spots on the ceilings.

Although I hate living in a trailer, we have more space than we did in Mr. Ferguson's house. My brothers and I sleep on bunk beds with the two of them on the bottom and me on the top. Privacy is still nonexistent. The next-door neighbor's front door is about thirty feet from our windows.

The wobbly doors freeze and do not shut properly. The pipes underneath our trailer are not insulated and burst each winter. Basically, it's better than a cardboard box, but not by much.

About the only good thing I can find is that we live within walking distance of my junior high school.

Soon I discover that Charles Roth teaches taekwondo and judo classes every Tuesday night in the school gym. Although the class is only for adults, my little brother and I start hanging around, longing for Mr. Roth to notice us. He's a stocky man with bushy eyebrows, a strong jaw, and big hands that are rough like sandpaper—probably from his work as a carpenter and construction worker.

"Mom, can I take karate class at the gym next door?" I ask.

"Now, Mark, you know we can't afford something like that," she says flatly in that tone of hers that tells me the case is closed.

One night Dale and I watch them break boards with one punch of their fists. I work up my courage and ask, "Mr. Roth, could Dale and I take your class?"

"Sorry, boys. This class if for adults only," he says gruffly. "We don't take kids."

We are back for the next class the following Tuesday, hanging out, watching from the shadows. Mr. Roth is a big-hearted, religious man with three daughters. He isn't used to how persistent a determined boy can be. Over the next month I pester him relentlessly to take us on.

Finally, one evening after class, I screw up my courage and ask again. "We'll do anything you say, Mr. Roth," I plead. "Just give us a chance. We'll work hard."

This humble man, who has become my idol, stares at me for a long minute and then says, "I'm not promising anything, but let me see what I can do."

He approaches the community college sponsoring the program and gets permission to extend the class to neighborhood children ages twelve and up. "I'll let you take the class, but your brother is too young," says Mr. Roth. "And I don't want any argument about it."

My brother Dale, eight, and I are tight. He follows me everywhere. My joy at getting a *yes* is temporarily dampened by Mr. Roth turning away Dale.

"Don't worry, Dale. I'll teach you everything I learn," I say, throwing my arm around his scrawny shoulders.

Next comes the hurdle of convincing my mom to give me money to pay for my uniform and my belt. I beg and plead until finally she gives me the fifteen dollars I need for my official *gei* and for the first three months of lessons. I proudly present Mr. Roth my crumpled dollar bills at the class the next night. He takes the wad, arranges the bills neatly with George Washington facing up, and carefully counts them one by one.

I am hungry to learn and cannot get enough of the sport. I finally have an outlet to channel my energy and my pent-up frustration.

I soak up everything I can from Mr. Roth, and then go home and demonstrate all the moves to my little brother. From a garage sale, I buy a small, gray wrestling mat for three dollars. We put it outside the trailer, and every night Dale and I spend hours practicing and working out together, often well beyond dark. I bring home the pieces of broken boards, and we break them until they are in too small of pieces to break any more.

I soon realize that Dale is progressing faster than me. *He really gets this*, I think, taking pride in his rapid progression. We ask Dale's twin brother, Kayle, if he wants to work out with us, but he shakes his head no and backs away like he's seen a rattlesnake. He goes back to his drawing. He's a gifted artist who constantly has a pencil in his hand, sketching. He takes after our paternal grandfather, who wrote and illustrated books.

Dale and I bond over taekwondo.

Eventually I decide it's high time Mr. Roth sees what Dale can do. I say, "My brother wants to work out with us."

He takes one look at the scrawny eight-year-old standing in front of him and says, "Oh, he's way too little. Look how little he is. He's a pint-sizer, little bitty, tiny kid."

Dale, small for his age and missing half a front tooth because a girl threw a phone that hit him in the mouth, brushes his long hair out of his eyes and looks up at Mr. Roth with a glint of defiance.

"Dale," I say, "show him the first kata."

My brother dives right in and flawlessly does a kata, a series of karate moves.

My instructor's jaw drops. "How did he know that?"

"Because we've been working out every day for hours after I go home."

He rubs the stubble of his five-o'clock shadow and says, "Tell you what, boys. You both come back next Tuesday."

Before long, Mr. Roth asks us to stay a few minutes after class. "I want you to come with our team to the next tournament," he says.

I feel a thrill at the prospect of getting to travel somewhere and show off what I've learned. But just as quickly, I worry about the entry fees for the tournament.

I jump up and down and then I bow deeply to Mr. Roth as I try to contain my excitement.

At my first tournament, held at Jefferson College in Hillsboro, Missouri, I take first place in my age group. Soon after, Dale starts competing as well. The Green brothers get so good, so fast that our mentor starts referring to us as champions. We quickly advance through the belt ranks—white, then yellow, then orange, then green, next blue, red, and brown until we earn our coveted black belts. Every time we progress to a new level, our mom grimaces, because she knows she'll have to fork out the fee for belts for each of us.

I crave the approval I see in Mr. Roth's eyes when he watches us spar. When I spar with him, he's like hitting a brick wall. He never gives an inch.

We work harder at taekwondo than anything we've ever done. Mr. Roth inspires me, coaches me, encourages me, and brings me down a notch or two whenever needed. I adopt him as a father figure.

By the next summer, he tells us, "For every time you win first place at a tournament, I will pay your entry fees into the next one."

He has to put his money where his mouth is, because we both win in our age groups in every tournament we enter. We travel all over the Midwest, eventually amassing 178 trophies between the two of us.

Whenever we enter the place where a competition is being held, we hear other competitors muttering, "The Green brothers are here." We become well-known on the tournament circuit.

The national championships take place in Peoria, Illinois, and I've fought my way to an invitation by age fourteen. In the final fight for the national title for my age group, I fight my heart out, but my best isn't quite good enough that day. I am awarded the silver medal. Mr. Roth is proud of me, and knowing that I can achieve something on that level sends my confidence soaring.

Eventually, our mom gets tired of dusting the trophy collection we've amassed. She throws her dust rag and yells for both of us: "Mark and Dale, get these things out of our house!"

She makes us gather them all up, and we take them to Mr. Roth, who in exchange for the trophies—which he recycles to other students with new labels—pays for karate camp for both Dale and me.

Even with the evidence of all of our victories gone, nobody can take away that powerful sense memory I have of what being a winner feels like. I decide that no matter what it takes, I never, ever want to come in second place again. I determine that I will be the absolute best at whatever I do.

CHAPTER FOUR

CHAOS

The reason people find it so hard to be happy is that they always see the past better than it was, the present worse than it is, and the future less resolved than it will be.

—Marcel Pagnol

Mom quits the donut shop once Kmart opens nearby. She lands a job working in the women's clothing department, taking home one hundred dollars a week. All day long she counts the items women are bringing into the dressing room, and then hangs up their unwanted castoffs.

The older we get, the wilder all of us become, and I am the ringleader. One weekend when Mom is gone—working a twelve-hour shift followed by a date—I throw a keg party funded by my cache of five-dollar bills that I regularly snatch each week from a worn manila envelope she keeps in her purse filled with cash and coins from that week's paycheck.

She asks me about it every week, too, but I lie straight to her face. "Nope, I didn't touch your purse," I declare, adopting a hang-dog look and acting hurt that she'd think such a thing. I can't explain the deadness I feel. I hate the feeling I get in the pit of my stomach. I try to justify it to myself since Mom never gives us an allowance, but I know I am wrong.

One weekend I throw a party when she goes home to see her parents. We have the trailer spic and span by the time she gets home early, except for one thing: an empty keg on the living-room floor.

"No more parties, Mark," Mom says. "I am really disappointed in you. I can't watch you every second."

I resent only having hand-me-down clothes to wear. I grow my hair out to try and look cool. There's no money for haircuts anyway.

I am always scrambling to find odd jobs, eager for pocket money. I get one of my first jobs while hitchhiking. I meet the owner of an awning business looking for help putting up skirting and awnings on mobile homes.

I also work in the Luck family's fireworks stand in the summer. They have a complete warehouse filled with fireworks. The Luck family has two brothers around my age. They sometimes get the key to the warehouse, and we help ourselves to some fireworks and set them off.

The family treats me like a son. I show up early for work, and their mom always feeds me breakfast. She is extra nice to me. I think she knows I come from one of those families who only gets Christmas if it's delivered in a Salvation Army truck and that our food comes with those white USDA government labels on it.

I find reasons to spend time at their house, which always smells like homecooked food. She makes me feel welcome and almost makes me feel like a third son.

Once, we are ice-skating on the pond in a valley far down below their house. The ice is not as thick as it needs to be, but it holds us. We dare each other to skate across it. Their Doberman Chopper chases us, nipping at our heels as we fly across the ice. You can see the water and ice shifting under our weight each time we go across.

On one of the passes, we hear a terrifying pop as loud as the firecrackers their family sells. Then we watch in horror as the oldest brother, Jim, falls through the ice. He immediately panics, and so do we.

His brother and I are the only two there. I get down on the ice on my belly and shimmy toward him. His brother grabs my ankles so I don't fall through, too. I stretch my hands out toward him as far as I can, and he locks his hands around my wrists. But the ice begins to crack and sink around me, forcing us to back off.

Finally, Jim figures out that he can break the ice by using his forearms and elbows. Like a human icebreaker, he slowly moves toward the shoreline. We race to pull him out. Hypothermia is swiftly setting in. His clothes are soaking wet. His brother and I both take one arm, and we help him up the hill together.

I learn something about myself that day. I am not a coward. If one of my friends is in trouble, I will sacrifice everything to make sure that person is safe. My whole life I've been told I'm no good and that I'm never going to amount to anything. But in that moment, I catch a glimpse of who I can be when the circumstance calls for it. And I like that guy.

***

When I am fourteen years old, an uncle of the Luck family hires me to help build a roof on a cement-block building. My job is to hook the metal beams one by one onto the boom to lift them into place. They are stacked on a truck with a wall behind me. I hook the first one on and when it begins lifting up, the force of the beam pushes the one under it off.

The metal beam heads straight for me. I jump backward off the truck with my back pressed against the wall. The enormous beam knocks me to the ground, pinning me with its crushing weight across both my legs. I feel the worst pain of my life. One leg goes numb and both immediately swell up and start to bruise. It's the first time in my life where I really experience that kind of pain.

Mom takes me to the hospital for x-rays. Turns out I don't have any broken bones, just severe bruising. Mom glosses over the whole incident because "Those folks are friends of ours, and they've been so nice to you. Besides, I don't need any kind of trouble."

While Mom wants to avoid trouble at all costs, if there is trouble to get into, I am in it. I start with petty stuff like putting coins in the carwash hoses by our house and watching them dance around due to the pressure, and lighting M-80s in culverts causing a huge percussion.

By age fifteen I drink pony Millers, Boone's Farm, and Mad Dog 20/20, hang out, and play foosball. I hitchhike on the roads between St. Louis and Jefferson Counties since I am not old enough to drive or own a car. I am never at home, and those rare times I do come home, I breeze in at all times of the night and day.

I never bother bringing home my report card. It's all buckshots and Fs or barely passing grades anyway.

Mom, Kayle, Mark, Dale, Audrey, Kelly, and Kristie

CHAPTER FIVE

SEARCHING

If you think you are beaten, you are;
If you think you dare not, you don't.
If you'd like to win, but think you can't
It's almost a cinch you won't.
If you think you'll lose, you've lost,
For out in the world we find
Success being with a fellow's will;
It's all in the state of mind.

If you think you're outclassed, you are:
You've got to think high to rise.
You've got to be sure of yourself before
You can ever win a prize.
Life's battles don't always go
To the stronger or faster man,
But soon or late the man who wins
Is the one who thinks he can.
—Walter D. Wintle

When summer break comes before my sophomore year, I tell my mom I've got something I've got to do. "I want to see my dad. I've saved enough money for a bus ticket."

"Why would you want to spend good money on a man who is no good?" she fires back.

I start to try to explain why I want to see the man who has been a blank for half my life, but then I stop. I can't even explain it to myself. "Don't worry, Mom. I won't be gone long," I say, giving her a kiss on the cheek.

After Dad left, we scarcely ever saw him again before he married the receptionist from New York Life and moved to El Paso, Texas.

I'd worked up the courage to call him a few weeks earlier to invite myself down for a visit. It was an awkward conversation punctuated with lots of long pauses. I hadn't really known what to say, and he didn't make it easy.

On the appointed morning, Mom gets up extra early to drop me off at the Greyhound bus station. On the thirty-hour bus ride stopping in every little town between Lake Charles and El Paso, I entertain myself as we get closer by counting tumbleweeds and jackrabbits. Once I finally arrive at the bus station, my dad picks me up in a shiny new car. His wife is gone the entire weekend, working. I never even see her. Dad ushers me to the guest room, where the Mexican maid has laid out fresh towels.

Although Dad is clean and sober, sipping on a Sprite constantly, I still desire a relationship but have zero emotional connection with him. By the time the weekend is over, I feel nothing. Just a numbness, a sort of gnawing pain in my gut knowing that my childish dream of having a dad who takes pride in me has died. I desperately try to hang on to those feelings, but they are as dead and dry as the tumbleweeds blowing across the highway in front of the bus.

On the long trip home, I start thinking about baseball. I don't even know where the ball he gave me is, and I've long since outgrown that glove.

***

By the time I turn sixteen and am a sophomore, I'm running with a rough crowd. I see my life spiraling in a direction I don't want it to go.

Northwest High School is in House Springs, nicknamed "Smoke City." Around that time, our town makes national news in the *New York Times*, which reports that a normal day for children here is to come home and see their "redneck" parents rolling up marijuana joints.

Most of the people I know have a patch of pot growing in their yards or in the woods nearby. Somebody in town makes up T-shirts celebrating that nickname, and those shirts become a hot commodity.

There are two groups at my high school. You are either part of the Burnouts or the Jocks. When I find myself totally disengaging from school and events, I realize in the end the people I am hanging with are only going to get me into more trouble.

As much as I dream about a future with Missouri in the rearview mirror, I still sometimes lapse into my old ways. One of the Luck boys and I decide in tenth grade that we are tired of Missouri and run away. We make it to Jefferson City, the state capital, ninety miles from home hitchhiking. The police pick us up. Mom can't afford the gas money to come get me, so she rides with the Lucks to come fetch us from the foster home where we've been assigned.

***

Something has to change and change fast. I get up early while Mom is getting ready for work and make a request: "Mom, could you call Mr. Ferguson and ask if we could use his address? I want to go to Eureka High School."

"Why? It's the middle of the school year, Mark."

"You know why, Mom. I just have a feeling something really bad is going to happen if I keep going to school in Jefferson County. I want to switch to Eureka. I need to get out of here. I can't handle this place."

What I leave unsaid but we both know is that on my current course right now the only thing I'm assured of is graduating to bigger and bigger trouble.

To my shock, she makes the call. An even bigger shock: Mr. Ferguson agrees to let us use his address.

In the mornings when Mom goes to work at 5:00 a.m., I ride with her and then walk to the bus stop next to Mr. Ferguson's house.

At Eureka High School I join the wrestling team. Since I'm still doing taekwondo—the only thing that gives me some security—I am confident that I can tackle that sport, too. After the first few practices, I make a decision. I want to get along with everyone, and I am able to move easily among all the high school cliques.

I hang around with the dive team, too, working out with them in the school pool. Soon my grades improve drastically, and I get Bs and Cs in most subjects.

I find reasons to stay at school. I avoid our trailer, because it's total chaos there: the drinking boyfriends, the dog no one picks up after, filthy carpets, and the grass so tall it almost hides our dry-rotted, underpinned trailer. Boys—most much bigger and older than me—hang around our trailer all the time, and my sisters pretty much ignore my efforts to protect them.

Sometimes I lapse into my old ways when it comes to school. My former stepbrother Gary—the second oldest and the only Ferguson I got along with—and I decide to ditch school one day to hang out in Babler State Park. There's a light dusting of snow on the ground. The roads in the park are glazed with a thin layer of ice. He loses control of the old beater he is driving, and we slam into a telephone pole, cracking it in half and shattering the front windshield. The park rangers arrive on the scene and call my former stepdad.

When he arrives, I recognize that familiar look in his eye when he's worked up about something. He doesn't speak to either of us while he hooks the car to his truck. We start to climb into the truck.

"Nope, you boys have another ride," he says, jerking his thumb toward the wrecked car. "Now get in."

The icy wind and shards of glass blow off the windshield and into our faces. After a few miles, he relents and lets us get back into the truck.

***

We've lived in the mobile home in Jefferson County for two years when Mom decides things aren't working out there like she'd hoped. "We're moving to St. Louis County," she says.

Maybe things are finally going to come together, I think, *since I'm already going to high school there anyway.*

She picks this little town by the Meramec River called Times Beach. The name is cool. I've always loved the water, so I'm really happy that we are moving. We swim the Meramec River as often as the weather allows.

She sells our old mobile home, and she uses what little money she gets to buy a new one. Besides a 7-11 grocery, a tiny post office, and a few small single-family houses, there isn't a whole lot to the town, which is really just a collection of trailer pads with a nice name.

Along with the lack of money, drugs and alcohol are just as bad here as in Smoke City. We're just in a different county.

My uncle comes over to do some favors around the house for my mom, takes one look around at her latest unkempt yard, a shed full of broken bikes, and non-working lawnmower. He says sharply, "You Green kids, you guys tear up everything. What's wrong with you anyway?"

Anytime Mom isn't around, he directs his displeasure at me for not keeping things up since I am the oldest boy. I am angry at myself but feel angry, too, at never having had a father around to teach me how to do anything.

His words sear into my brain. I want to shout back at him that we're just a bunch of kids and we didn't choose any of this. *Besides, as soon as I have my diploma, I'll be outta here so fast that you'll be choking on my dust.*

But instead I choke down the words and swallow my pride. Maybe he's right. Nothing good ever happens to us. I swear I can feel the bitterness filling up the hungry pit that no amount of government peanut butter and cheese can ever satisfy.

Because I had started taekwondo back in sixth grade, I am pretty good at it by now, having earned a brown belt. Thing is, when you live in the kind of places we always wind up, you almost have to be a scrapper. If you can't fight, people somehow smell that fear on you, and then you end up getting beat up. I learned to fight early on, and have the broken noses, black eyes, and stitches to show for it. I am always scrapping with somebody.

One night I am out with friends and my sister Kelly, and we somehow get in a fight with an older group of guys from Pacific, Missouri, underneath the Meramec River Bridge. I am in the middle of winning a fistfight with one of them when another takes a tire jack out of the trunk of his car. After the guy coldcocks me with the tire jack, I crumple to the rocks, unconscious.

I am bathed in white light and feel peaceful. Then suddenly I hear my sister's voice. I wake up in an ambulance. At the hospital, I get forty stitches in my cheek and neck. The doctor tells me I have a concussion. Once I can sit up straight, I call home and tell Mom what's happened.

"I'm sorry, son, but I haven't gotten paid yet this week, so I don't have the gas to come get you," she says. The gas embargo and rations have limited the amount of gas we can have and sent prices soaring to almost triple what they'd been. She barely has enough to make it to work each day as it is.

I can tell by the way her voice is shaking that she feels really bad about not being able to come. "It's okay, Mom," I say. "I'll hitch a ride home."

And I do. I hitch a ride to a truck stop off of I-44. A driver takes pity on me and drops me off on the highway median near Times Beach. Barefoot and in a bloody, stained T-shirt, my head throbs like nothing I've ever experienced. I am furious when I realize that the one new pair of Levis Mom just bought me for the school year is torn and soaked in blood. Getting a new pair of jeans each school year is one of the few things I look forward to.

That tire jack came within millimeters of piercing my aorta, but one thought loops over and over through my addled brain: *And now my brand-new pair of Levis is ruined.*

***

One Saturday afternoon, I come across some of my buddies down by the railroad tracks in Eureka. I can tell they've been drinking by their eyes, but nobody mentions that they've been hitting vodka hard since noon.

"C'mon, Green. We're just out for a little afternoon drive, so hop in," says my friend as he revs the engine on his Ford Pinto.

I laugh and shake my head.

"Don't be a chicken," he says when he sees my hesitation.

I can never resist any kind of challenge. Once I get in the car with him and his buddies, I realize how intoxicated they all are. The driver gets on Interstate 66, headed east, and soon he's speeding along at ninety miles per hour.

"Stop, stop, you've got to let me out," I yell.

But they just laugh and the driver shouts back, "We're going, we're going, going, gone!"

He puts on more gas, topping one hundred miles per hour. He swerves, narrowly missing a pickup truck. The angry driver starts chasing us for the next ten miles. In response, the driver's buddy lobs full cans of beer from the cooler at the truck tailing us.

Soon we are in the middle of a high-speed chase with a state trooper in hot pursuit. Finally, after almost crashing multiple times, my friend pulls over.

A police helicopter hovers overhead. The driver is handcuffed and carted off to jail while his passengers, including me, are instructed to lay face down on the hot asphalt with our hands above our heads while the trooper and local police sort out what to do with us.

My heart is pounding out of my chest. After what seems like hours, they hand each of us a seventy-five-dollar ticket for highway littering and let us go with a stern warning.

Our luck holds steady. Turns out Times Beach is situated in a flood zone, and it floods twice within the first year of our move. The National Guard is called in to save a bunch of people from drowning. On top of that, some unscrupulous business owner buys some contaminated oil from a company and sprays it all over the gravel streets in our town to settle the dust and dirt. The Environmental Protection Agency gets called in and declares our town a disaster zone from the dioxin coating our streets, so once again, we have to move. My mom accepts the settlement of $1,000 a person that the company offers.

She moves to an apartment by Busch Gardens—near the stables for the famed Clydesdales—because it's closer to her job at Kmart.

My little brother Dale, a high school freshman, and I both have our black belts and make it to the national championships in taekwondo that year. I don't win, but Dale takes second place in the nation, ensuring that he gets an invitation to join the Olympic team at its training camp in Colorado Springs. But my mom has to deliver the bad news that his Olympic dreams are out of reach for a family on food stamps. We don't know how to get sponsorships, and it never occurs to Mom to ask for help.

***

You'd think I'd learn a lesson about skipping school, but when it comes time for graduation and the annual tradition of Senior Skip Day, good intentions overcome my common sense.

A bunch of us guys and girls spend the day drinking, and by early evening we pile into our friend's GTO and head back to the high school. The driver decides to pull into the school courtyard. It is drizzling rain, and the grass in the courtyard is wet. There is a covered breezeway between the two administration buildings on either side of the large grass courtyard.

Somebody yells, "Let's cut a doughnut!"

Pretty soon the whole carload of us is egging him on. He starts out on a concrete area at one end and accelerates until we hit the grass. The driver turns the wheel, but his bald tires combined with the slick wet grass send us straight into the breezeway pole at about fifteen miles per hour.

The collision pierces the radiator, and steam is coming out. The front hood and front bumper are smashed, and my friend's beloved car is toast. He starts crying.

As luck would have it, the janitor just so happens to still be at the school.

The next morning, we are all called into the principal's office. I am two weeks away from getting my diploma from Eureka High School. I am part of a work program where I get two credits for being in it. I need those two credits to graduate. When the teacher learns about our escapade, she drops me from the course two weeks before graduation. I am stunned and ashamed.

I know my mom won't take time off from work to go fight their decision. None of the other kids in that car suffer that kind of punishment. I'm the only one who sits in study hall for the final two weeks of school, knowing I'm not walking across that stage and getting my diploma. Since I make that decision to stick it out, I get a certificate stating that I attended twelve years of school.

All my friends graduate. I don't.

That's it. Twelve years and all I've got to show for it is a certificate saying that I attended, which as far as I'm concerned is the equivalent of acknowledging that I am alive but that nothing I do counts. Ever.

CHAPTER SIX

GYPSIES, TRAMPS, AND THIEVES

We are products of our past, but we don't have to be prisoners of it.

—Rick Warren

What am I doing? My life is a mess. There has got to be a better way. I am walking along the side of the road, wondering what on earth I'm going to do. All I can think about is hightailing it out of Missouri and getting a fresh start. *Well okay, so here I am. I'm eighteen years old. I got nothing, I got nobody, I got adversity and mess all around me. Why not just go?*

For a decade, I've been nursing a big, wide, gaping wound of abandonment and grief over my dad. My anger and bitterness are at a constant boil just under the surface.

Even when I'm trying to keep it together, trouble always finds me. One evening I am drunk from downing a six-pack with a small group of my buddies when we run into this group of guys we call "Hoosiers." It's a label that means somebody who is dirty, unkempt, and outside the mainstream. They drive past in a filthy, old beater pickup. Anytime we cross paths, we wind up squaring off.

As soon as we see them drive by, we jump in my girlfriend's Jeep and give chase. The fight is on. They wheel into this small rundown neighborhood, and I catch one of the guys on the front porch of this ramshackle house and start wailing on him.

He manages to run inside the front door and lock it. In my drunken state, I decide to use my taekwondo skills against four small plate-glass windows in the front of the house. *Pow! Pow! Pow! Pow!* They all shatter against my fist.

That'll teach him to mess with me.

I look down and realize that I have cuts on both hands, my wrist, and my thumb. I'm bleeding all over the place. We take off, and a couple minutes away, we get pulled over.

"Step out of the car, boys," says the Deputy Sheriff of St. Louis County. "Everybody show me your hands."

As soon as I hold my hands up, I get cuffed and the officer hauls me off to jail after a quick stop at the hospital to get me stitched up. The charge is property damage, a misdemeanor. I'm there overnight, and then they release me on my own recognizance. I have a court date. I get put on probation and told not to leave the state.

***

Two weeks later, the answer to my unspoken prayer comes in the form of a phone call.

"How would you like to make a hundred dollars a day?" my friend asks.

"What? Okay, what are we going to do? Sell drugs? What's the kicker?"

He laughs and replies, "I was hitchhiking on I-70 and these guys in a dump-truck caravan picked me up. They are looking for help to lay blacktop. The boss told me he could use me and asked if I had any friends who'd want to do it, too. The job's in Arkansas."

My mind is spinning. *Arkansas is definitely not the same state as Missouri. I have a choice to make. I can work, make good money, and then maybe try and get myself out of this mess later. Or, I can stay in St. Louis in the situation I'm in with the people I hang around with and the things that are going on, and there's no telling what can happen.*

"You know what, partner? I'm out of here," I say. "When do we leave?"

"Pull your stuff together. Come to the motel where we are staying."

My friend and I drive over to this rundown motel, meet the boss, and ask a few questions. I go home and toss a few of my belongings into a garbage bag and meet up at the motel again. I ride in that big dump truck all the way to Arkansas. *Figures that this would be my ride to a new life.*

After we cross the state line into Arkansas, I start asking questions about the crew. I quickly learn that my new employers are gypsies. They have their own language and their own rules. Nonetheless, I have to leave. I couldn't stay. I know in my bones that if I stay in Missouri, there is going to be no life for me.

For the next eighteen months, we go off on trips all over the Southeast and the Midwest and lay blacktop. Whenever we aren't on the road, I live in an eight-by-ten shed next to the railroad tracks. I'm one of the few outsiders. When we're in the gypsy camp, the women cook one meal a day for us. Sometimes I use my money to buy some extra grub.

The gypsies are a tightly knit group, but usually not honest people. It isn't uncommon for them to steal from each other and us. Sometimes they do some petty theft while we are out on the road all across Texas, Alabama, Mississippi, and Tennessee.

In the winter, they let us build a fire. We sit outside next to the railroad tracks and drink Jack Daniels straight from a bottle that we pass around while we swap stories.

When we work, we work hard. Our days are twelve-hour shifts with a short break for lunch. We keep the trucks clean and the equipment running. I learn a skill and how to drive a truck in the process. They pay us every day. That's one promise they keep.

Every once in a while, the boss lets us drive the dump truck into town. My buddy and I pull up to this pool hall in our borrowed wheels one night. I walk in, and I see this girl who is managing the place. She's cute and confident and a little bit sassy. I like her confidence and the fact that she doesn't take any guff off of anybody. I don't know what possesses me to say it, but I just look at my buddy and say, "I'm going to marry her."

I flirt with her and ask her if she'd like to go out. "I'll pick you up in my dump truck," I say.

She bats her big eyes at me, laughs, and says, "That'll be fine."

I pick her up the next night and take her to the drive-in movie in my dump truck. We have to park on the back row, but she doesn't mind.

One night while we're out in the dump truck right near my shack in the gypsy camp, one of the two gas tanks on the truck shows flat empty. I know with a flick of the switch that I can use the other tank, but instead I say, "We're out of gas. I guess you'll have to stay the night."

After we've dated a few months, Jennie gives me an ultimatum: "It's the gypsies or me."

We're both barely twenty years old. I have no idea what I'll do for work if I quit my steady job with the gypsies. It's decision time.

I need a new job, but I can't find anything, so my girlfriend, my friend from the gypsy camp, and I have a 1956 Chrysler that barely runs and use an Arkansas gas card—a piece of garden hose—to syphon enough gas to get us to Florida.

We wind up in Lakeland, Florida. Once we park the car, it never moves again. I get a job tearing down an old house and then one as a house painter. She can't find anything, so we survive on Snickers and oranges. At times, we are so strapped for cash and so hungry that we sell plasma to the local blood bank.

I hit rock bottom and call my dad to ask if he'll send some money via Western Union. He tells me to go to the YMCA.

We somehow manage to make it back to Arkansas and move in with her parents. When I tell my buddy that I'm thinking of asking her to marry me, he looks at me like I've lost my mind and says, "Don't do it."

I ignore him, and we never see each other again.

My girlfriend and I decide to get married. I go to downtown Pine Bluff and pay two hundred dollars for a diamond ring.

We say "I do" in front of her parents' fireplace. I'd picked out what I thought was a nifty looking, plaid, nylon shirt for five dollars at a garage sale. I wear it and feel good about how I look that day. She wears a simple white dress.

We move into a tiny efficiency apartment, the kind where you pull the bed out of the wall and into the living room. Then her uncle, who works for a plant that manufactures fifty-five-gallon drums, tells me about a job in that place. I get the job, and I work there for six months, loading these sixteen-gauge drums that weigh fifty pounds each into a truck. Two other guys and I stack the drums three deep, row by row until the truck is full.

It is back-breaking work physically, but what gets to me is the mind-numbing boredom of it. I've always had a short attention span and hate repetition.

I land a job on a garbage truck. I figure it's better than nothing. But at night, I toss and turn. I think, *Okay, I'm out of here too. I'm not doing this.*

I can't get started on anything that feels like I'm building toward a future. I've failed to find that second chance at life, and it is really depressing. But I can't just leave. *I'm married now. I'm going to make a life for us somehow.*

Soon after, my wife tells me she's pregnant. *If I'm going to be a dad and have a family to support, I can't work on a garbage truck.* I get this idea and tell her, "If I go back and clean up my record, the Army will take me."

I go to the recruiting station and shoot straight with the recruiter: "Hey, you know, I got in trouble. What should I do to get this right so I can join the service? I want to be in the Army."

After looking over a list of job positions, I tell him I want to be a machinist. I know my uncle makes good money, and that's one of the few jobs I'm familiar with on the list he hands me.

But then the next guy I meet with tells me the only opening is for a welder. I buck up and insist that I want to be a machinist. I'm tired of other people deciding my fate.

"Sorry, but all we've got right now is a welder, buddy. Take it or leave it."

I shrug and walk out. The recruiter's mouth drops open in shock. It feels good to take a stand for what I want for once.

I go back to my humdrum job for the next three months. Then the recruiter calls and says, "We've got an opening for the job you want."

"Okay. Good, let's go." I get a glimmer of hope that my life can finally change.

He says, "All you got to do is go fix your problem back in Missouri, and then we can get you signed up."

A few nights later after a couple of beers, I decide it's now or never. I kiss my wife, rub her baby bump, and say, "I'm going back and fixing this so we can have a life."

I put on my straw hat and my cowboy boots, and I hop in my old '65 Chevy step-side pickup truck. It only hit on six of its eight cylinders, but it gets me where I want to go. Winter has come, and it's a nippy forty degrees outside and my heater is on the blink. But off I go.

I drive until I hit the Missouri border, shortly before midnight. Just as I cross the state line, blue lights come up fast behind me. God is not wasting any time.

What the hell? I think. *How did he know to pull me over? I know I wasn't speeding. How long has it been since my last beer?*

The officer walks up, and I roll the window down. A blast of cold air hits me in the face. I am already cold, because my heater's not working, but now I'm shivering from the cold and fear.

"Are you aware that your left taillight is out, young man?" he asks. I shake my head no, afraid he'll smell the alcohol on my breath. "Let me see your driver's license and registration," he commands. I hand him both, trying to steady my trembling hands. I don't have insurance. He says, "I'll be right back." When he returns, he says, "You need to step out of the truck."

You know that's trouble when you hear those words.

Since I'd left the state while I was on probation for the misdemeanor of property damage from when I broke windows during a fight, there is an active warrant out for my arrest. He hauls me to St. Louis County, and I'm escorted to a holding cell in a prison called Gumbo Bottoms, an ominous-looking place with razor wire topping its tall fences. I spend a week in a minimum-security holding-cell area with juveniles and troublemakers. My brain is on overload, so I can scarcely think.

A few days later, they bus a group of us to the courthouse. Finally, a guard calls my name and takes me before a judge. When my name comes up on the docket, I stand in my bright-orange jumpsuit before the St. Louis County Court Judge, who asks, "Okay, so what's going on?"

"Well, Your Honor, I'm joining the Army," I reply. "I'm getting the paperwork together, and I came back to Missouri because I need a new life, and I need a second chance at things, and I want to get out of here. And I'm going to sign, and I can't do that until this is cleared up."

He peers at me from his glasses and then examines my paperwork. After what seems an eternity, he looks me straight in the eye and says, "All right. Get out of here. I don't ever want to see you in my courtroom again."

"Yes, sir, Your Honor. You don't have to worry about that," I answer. I'm happy because I stood and faced adversity, and I tell myself, "You know what? I can overcome this."

As I'm escorted back to my cell, I can't stop smiling. *All right, you know, maybe things are going to start turning around for me.* I'm elated that something's going to change for the positive now, because I'll have a job, I'll have a trade, I'll have a future, I can go to school, and I can do all kinds of things. I'm excited about life for the first time in a long time.

CHAPTER SEVEN

ATTITUDE ADJUSTMENT

Choosing one's attitude in a given set of circumstances is the last of human freedoms. You can take away emotion, love, comforts, inflict pain, and remove freedom but the attitude of a man is his savior or his failure.

—Victor Frankl

I have the release paperwork in my hand when the guard puts me back in my cell. I'm eager to hand it off to the office downstairs so I can get out of this place, but the stone-faced guard doesn't say anything, just turns the key and walks away.

"Hey. Hey, can you let me go make my phone call, so I can have somebody come pick me up as soon as we're done with all the release paperwork?" I call after him.

The guy ignores me. Acts like I don't exist.

I mean, who wants to be in a place like this anyway, stripped of your freedom? "Hey buddy," I call again, thinking maybe he didn't hear me.

No response. He just sits with his back to me.

My cheeks flush red, and my usual fight-or-flight trigger snaps. I get loud: "Hey dude, I want to make my phone call, so can you do something about it, please?" My patience and good mood evaporate. I've got my paperwork, and I'm supposed to be let go.

He gets on his radio.

"About damn time," I sputter, angrily pushing my long blond hair out of my eyes.

Then I hear him say, "We got one." He stays seated, never turning in my direction.

A couple minutes later this guard built like a pro football player comes pounding up the stairs. He wears that "I can take you down" look on his face. His hands look like meat cleavers, and I know in that instant that my mouthy, punk attitude has landed my five-foot-eight, 125-pound self in a world of trouble.

He fills up the entire door to my cell and then snatches it open. I notice a big, black two-way radio in his right hand. He grabs me by my hair with his left hand and slams his radio into the back of my head with his right hand over and over again. It all happens in slow motion, just like the night my dad left. Then he starts hitting me on the top of my head and then the sides. *He's avoiding my face, so this beating won't leave any marks.* I feel myself slipping into darkness.

I can't believe that ten minutes ago I was excited about going somewhere and going home, and now I'm afraid my life's about to end.

After he's beaten me down to the ground, he reaches behind me and yanks me up by my underwear, giving me a wedgie that's painful beyond description. He rips me up from my crumpled position on the floor and starts dragging me down the hallway, carrying most of my weight in his right hand. My toes are barely touching the concrete floor. A couple more inches, and I swear I could pull my underwear over the top of my head and read the label.

Once we reach the stairs, he abruptly lets me go while simultaneously giving me a slight shove. As I tumble down the stairs, he calls out, "Whoops, sorry, fella."

In a flash, this six-foot-four monster of a man is beside me, yanking me to my feet and hauling me down the next long hallway. He stops, slams me up against the wall, and presses his barrel chest into mine so forcefully I can scarcely draw a breath. He screams inches from my face exactly what a piece of garbage I am, following up with: "You're wasting my time, and I should just throw you in the hole."

I have no idea what or where the hole is. Although I wouldn't mind being swallowed up in a hole right about now, I don't think I want to find out about the one he's talking about. With all my near-death experiences, I've never been scared out of my mind . . . I guess because normally I hadn't come across a situation where I wasn't pretty certain I could come out on top. But this guy shows me in the span of a few minutes that I'm not nearly as tough as I think I am. Being a black belt in taekwondo in this situation means diddly squat.

He keeps yelling with a voice like a foghorn, one long continuous blast of all the horrible things I've heard about myself my whole life. All the while, he forces me to look him in the eye. I swear his eyes glow red with fire in them.

The blood drains from my face, and I'm so scared my face goes numb. It tingles and feels like ants are crawling all over it like when the bad guys torture the good guys with fire ants in those old black-and-white Westerns I used to watch.

I can't help it when the tears start to flow.

All of a sudden, he stops and asks my name.

"Mark, my name's Mark," I whisper, still shaking and wiping the wetness off my face.

"Why are you here?"

I tell him my story in as few words as possible, fearful of setting him off again. When I mention my plan of joining the Army, I see his jaw relax slightly.

"Why didn't you tell me that in the first place?" he says, breaking into a smile. "I was in the Corps. Have you considered the Marines?"

I am stunned. Then we both laugh. I answer cautiously, "No, sir, I gave my word to the Army recruiter. I've already got a job lined up as a machinist."

"Well then, let's get this paperwork done and get you out of here, boy."

"Sure, sir. I mean, yes, sir. That would be great."

Once the paperwork is finally finished a half hour later, I think I'm scot free. The jailer hands me back my street clothes, my wallet, and the keys to my canary-yellow truck, which had been impounded when I was arrested.

"One more thing, boy," he says. "I see here you've got an outstanding ticket for littering a highway on your record. You better get that taken care of right away, so you don't wind up seeing us again."

He hands me over to the local police from Times Beach, which is where the first beer can was thrown from the car. I ride to the police station, settle up, and walk outside.

I am exuberant. *I am free. I have my liberty back. I am free to do what I want with my life. I have my second chance.*

As the sun breaks through the overhanging gray clouds on that December morning, I declare out loud to the cold winter wind whipping around me and to myself, "No one from this point forward is ever going to stop me from excelling at everything that I ever choose to do. And no one is ever going to stop me or tell me I cannot do something. And no one ever again has the right to put limitations on me."

Then I take my paperwork to the Army recruitment station in St. Charles, Missouri, and sign up. I'm given a deferred entry for March, three months out.

CHAPTER EIGHT

AIRBORNE

Always remember that your own resolution to succeed is more important than anything else.

—Abraham Lincoln

When I get off the plane to take a bus to the eight-week basic training camp in Fort Dix, New Jersey, I don't have anything to my name.

It's thirty degrees outside, the bus is unheated, and I'm freezing. I don't own a jacket. I have the T-shirt I'm wearing, my jeans are full of holes, and my socks reek. I can't remember ever having the money to pay a barber for a real haircut, so my hair is long and shaggy.

All I have is my pregnant wife a thousand miles away back in Arkansas and the possibility of a future if I handle myself right over the next nine months in this camp.

We sleep in the barracks. I scarcely sleep a wink due to the stress. The first formation that next morning is outside. I'm the only guy in the entire platoon without a coat on. The drill sergeant comes up and stands in front of me and asks, "Where is your coat?"

I say the first thing that pops in my mind. "Drill Sergeant, I was told the Army's going to give me everything."

"That doesn't include a coat," he replies. After a beat, he adds, "You get inside and get yourself a coat. Go and tell that charge of quarters in there to get you a coat."

I do as he instructed, and the charge of quarters is looking for a field jacket or a jacket of any kind. The only thing he can find is a long, black, London Fog raincoat with a wide collar and a thin belt attached to the waist.

I put it on, thankful for any kind of layer to ward off the bone-chilling cold of a New Jersey winter morning, and head back outside to reclaim my spot in the formation. I stand at attention, my long hair flapping in the wind along with my coattails, and the drill sergeant says, "You look like a drug dealer."

Everybody within earshot of our exchange snickers and tries to muffle their laughter.

I smile, too. "I guess I probably do look like a drug dealer, sir, but I hope to have that remedied soon," I say.

I make a new friend, Dwayne Riden, who shares the Bible with me. My parents sometimes took us to church when I was little, but that stopped when he left. Shortly before I finish basic training, I get baptized.

We have a briefing to ensure there are no felons among us. One of the officers says, "If you have ever done anything you did not tell us, you need to come clean now."

My hands get sweaty, and my mind is spinning. I told the recruiter everything, and he assured me I was good to go. *But what if that isn't good enough? It's now or never.*

I decide not to take any chances. I raise my hand and they signal me to come out of formation. My new background check shows that I am clean, and I am told that I am not in any trouble and to rejoin the formation.

I am relieved but also proud. It feels good to take responsibility and do the right thing.

After I complete basic training, I get my advanced individual training (AIT) for my assigned job. I'm in a night study class, because the Army, Navy, Air Force, and Marines all studied to be machinists in the same building, so we had to split the hours into twelve-hour shifts. I finish AIT, get my job, and then I hear they are looking for volunteers for Airborne. "What's the benefit of going Airborne?" I ask.

"Well, you get some pride," my commanding officer answers. "You are part of a rapid-deployment force fighting for your country. There's a lot of prestige associated with the 82nd Airborne and the 101st Airborne Divisions."

For me, the kicker is that if you are a junior enlisted soldier, you can stay stateside with your family. Whereas if you are in another division, and you get orders to Germany, you have to pay for your family to get there—something I know I cannot afford.

When I hear those benefits, I think, *Well, I'm not going to leave my wife. She's having a baby.* I volunteer for Airborne. I know it is going to be tough and a real challenge. You've got to have paperwork to make sure you're healthy enough to endure jumping out of airplanes and landing on the ground like a sack of potatoes. I make an appointment to go meet this doctor for my Airborne physical.

I walk into this small clinic with my paperwork in my hand. This grizzled old doctor looks me over, then asks in a gruff voice, "Are you healthy?"

"Yeah, I'm healthy," I say.

"Give me the damn paperwork."

He signs off on everything, and out the door I go.

When I leave for jump school in Fort Benning, Georgia, I quickly learn why the 82nd Airborne has such a stellar reputation. They run you to death.

Your legs are like steel when you leave there. You learn how to fall, you learn how to land, and you learn how to turn a parachute properly, so you don't run with the wind and go twice as fast before you hit. They teach you how to check your equipment. It's laser-focused and all business.

In the aircraft, you've got to pay attention on how you're getting up, how you're checking your stuff, and how you're getting out the door, because when you go out the door of that plane, there ain't no coming back. Your stuff has got to be right.

At Fort Benning, they call Tac Sergeants the Black Hats. On the first week, we get so much physical training that my body is limp sore from so much lactic acid buildup.

Next the Black Hats drive into us on the mental side. "Today we're going to show you how you're going to take a break," one of the biggest Black Hat trainers says. "And we're going to teach you where you need to be, when you need to be there, and there's not going to be anybody being late."

Then without giving further instruction, they stand off to the side and huddle up with six of them in a circle talking.

Some of the guys who came for training were smokers. The Black Hats had pointed to where the break area is going to be, but never say when the break will be.

One of the recruits is obviously having a fit to have a cigarette, so he walks over right by the edge of where the Black Hats had indicated the break area is and proceeds to light up. Well, once one does, another one wants to light up. The next thing you know everybody who smokes is in a little huddle. Once that happens, gradually everybody else starts gravitating toward the break area until we are all over there.

The next thing we know, six Black Hats are screaming at the top of their lungs for us to put our feet up on the trees and start doing pushups. Then we do leg lifts, and then we do more pushups, and then we do jumping jacks, and every other exercise you can imagine for almost two hours straight. They are testing our mettle to see what we are made of. It takes a certain kind of soldier to be tough enough to meet the demands of being an Airborne soldier.

When you're tested in life, you've got to decide how tough you're going to be, and whether you're going to fight back and stay in there, and fight and give it what you got. The end result of giving up during training is that you're going home, and you won't be an Airborne soldier. You're not going to be able to wear the pride of those wings. You're going to have to go back and explain to somebody you love why you couldn't hack it.

If someone gets hurt, the others deride that trainee for being lame and lazy—even if the reason you're hurt isn't your fault. There are three absolutes for Airborne:

1. You have to be healthy,
2. you have to be physical,
3. and you have to be ready at all times.

After we finally finish that marathon exercise session, about a dozen of the recruits cop serious attitudes and give up. The Black Hats just keep right on coming at us. They roll right over those guys.

They quit, and the Black Hats send them to what they call the white house, where they are processed out. Then they are gone.

The rest of us stay. We wake up the morning after the bloodletting to the sound of one of the Black Hats kicking a trash can down the hall and screaming at the top of his lungs for us to get outside on the double.

We run several miles a day. We push all the time to get strong, to be ready, to train, to do the right things, and to listen. That's one of the main things I learn in Airborne training—the importance of listening. When you put your life in the hands of others and vice versa when jumping out of a perfectly good airplane, you have to be a good listener. Landing safely from a jump hinges on listening and paying attention to detail.

After four weeks of training and enduring test after test to weed out the weak, I graduate from Airborne training and receive my orders for the 82nd Airborne in Fort Bragg, North Carolina. The All Americans, as the division is known, is famed for the tremendous adversity endured in France during World War II. Ever since, the 82nd Airborne has stood ready as America's guard and has been the first division to jump into dangerous areas and take care of the country's business.

***

I've been sending home money every month for my wife to deposit in our joint checking account to provide for her and our new baby girl. Things are finally falling into place, and I am proud of correcting the course I was on.

With my first three-day leave, I head straight for Arkansas. I cannot wait to see Jennie. I decide to surprise her.

She's surprised, all right. I follow her to a bar, where it's obvious that I've been replaced. She's left our little girl with her mom. I wait for her back at the house, and while I'm waiting, I build a rocking cradle for our baby Stephanie.

When Jennie comes home, her eyes widen with shock at the sight of me. I notice that her wedding ring is missing. "That money you've been sending home didn't go very far," she says, and then adds that she pawned her ring. She might as well have punched me in the gut.

I tell her that I'll be filing for divorce as soon as I get back to my base. She looks at me with dead eyes.

I stay up all night painting the cradle for our tiny daughter. I am in shock that my marriage is over before it really got started. Tears stream down my face with each brushstroke of pink paint.

The next day, I leave to go back to the base. The first thing I do is head to the military's Staff Judge Advocate at Fort Bragg. He draws up the paperwork for the divorce. Forty dollars later, I'm a single man again.

I am twenty-one years old. I'm divorced and have a baby girl, Stephanie, whom I've scarcely seen.

***

On one of the night jumps in the 82nd Airborne, I jump out of the plane, and after my chute deploys, I realize something is not right. My chute is dropping quicker than usual. Then I recognize that the jumper underneath me is stealing my air. Within seconds I find myself tangled up in the suspension lines of the other jumper's chute.

Somehow, I manage to kick my legs free just as we approach the ground. I hit the ground much harder than a normal jump, but luckily I am not injured and neither is he.

The lesson: You have to somehow muster up the strength to continue forward and not let it shake you when things go terribly wrong.

CHAPTER NINE

WARRIOR ATHLETE

A black belt is a white belt who never quit.
—Senior Grand Master Edward B. Sell

Now that I am stationed at Fort Bragg, I start to feel a connection, a sense of purpose and accomplishment that I've craved. Our schedules are brutal, but the camaraderie and the feeling of being part of a world-class team go a long way toward making it bearable. Maybe because I experienced virtually no discipline growing up, I thrive on the challenge and certainty of it.

Men, whom I can genuinely say I admire, surround me. Something about standing on a parade field with eighteen thousand paratroopers during All American Week gives you a new kind of confidence. The mix of people from all over the United States, all focused on one mission of defending our country, and the friendships born out of extreme training and hard work stay with you for a lifetime. I am a part of a band of brothers all committed to the defense of our country. I feel a sense of pride of being part of the one of the Army's most elite divisions.

I see the confidence level of the noncommissioned officers, and I push myself to be like them. You learn to trust the parachute rigger who packed your parachute and has your life in his hands. You learn that you are part of a team committed to excellence. There is no room for a mistake once you step out of the door of an aircraft moving at hundreds of miles an hour.

***

Since that one disastrous visit with my dad when I was sixteen years old, I've only spoken to him a few times. He never calls or writes. If anybody is going to reach out, it's always on me. I try to reach him one time after I enlist, thinking that he'll be proud that I followed in his footsteps, but he never responds.

As much as I try to ignore that gnawing sense in my soul that I never quite measure up, that I'm destined to fail somehow, it overtakes me at random moments. The worst times are at night when I lay awake in my bunk. That's when my brain feels like it's on fire with thoughts racing. Flashes of my dad walking out that night and the parade of men who came in and out of my life steal what few hours I have before "Reveille" just before dawn breaks.

Sometimes I long to hear those notes, which signal that it's time to put on the uniform. When I'm in uniform, I do a better job of managing my own thoughts that wage war against me. I know exactly who I am, and I am part of something bigger.

I am a soldier.

***

One afternoon, I'm walking by the mess hall and see a note posted on the bulletin board by Specialist Pedro Laboy. The word *taekwondo* jumps out at me. I scan the flyer and learn that Laboy is trying to put together a team of soldiers to compete in the state championships.

I am rusty but in tip-top shape, thanks to all the constant training and running we do as part of our physical training in the Airborne. My legs are like steel. Up until joining Airborne, taekwondo is the only thing I've ever tried that made me feel like I was worth something.

The moment I read that note, I think of my mentor Senior Grand Master Edward Sell, whom I studied taekwondo with during my time in Lakeland, Florida. I spent a few short months working out with him in a small church that had a wood floor. I remember the sun gleaming through the stained-glass windows onto my uniform. It was quiet and small and was a great place to train. Learning the basics of meditation and having his leadership during those months proved to have a lasting effect on me.

During the Korean War, Senior Grand Master Sell was stationed in Korea with the Air Force. Americans were first introduced to the sport when Second Lieutenant Hong Hi Choi of the Korean Armed Forces instructed Korean Army troops along with American soldiers in the 2nd Infantry Division. Choi, who was promoted to General, attended Ground General School at Fort Riley near Topeka, Kansas, where he gave public demonstrations for our troops. The President of Korea sent Tae Hi Nam to Fort Benning, Georgia, for radio communications training, where Nam ended up giving many demonstrations of the sport, drawing large crowds. My mentor happened to be right in the middle of the start of what became modern-day taekwondo, which was introduced in the US by the military.

When I trained with Senior Grand Master Sell, he was the highest-ranking non-Asian black belt in the world, holding a ninth-degree black belt. I recently found out he was awarded his tenth-degree black belt by South Korea posthumously. Since being trained in Korea, he had returned there many times along with his wife, Brenda Sell, who is also a Grand Master with an eighth-degree black belt. He was the first coach of the US team in the first World Taekwondo Championship in Korea in 1973 and founded the Korean Taekwondo Association of America and Christian Taekwondo University, among several other organizations promoting the sport.

He heavily emphasized taekwondo's eleven rules in his school:

1. Loyalty to your country
2. Respect your parents
3. Faithfulness to your spouse
4. Loyalty to your friends
5. Respect your brothers and sisters
6. Respect your elders
7. Respect your teachers
8. Never take life unjustly
9. Indomitable spirit
10. Loyalty to your school
11. Finish what you begin

I stand there for several minutes, thinking about the many lessons I learned in my short time of training with Senior Grand Master Sell. Until I met the Senior Grand Master, I'd spent most of my life with the voice in my head being my enemy, magnifying every single bad decision I'd ever made. He taught me to meditate—how to clear, focus, and calm my mind, which I needed desperately. Too often my thoughts are as jumpy as the cottontail rabbits I used to chase as a kid in Missouri.

When I was baptized during basic training at Fort Dix, the Senior Grand Master was the person I wrote to share the good news, and he wrote me right back on June 23, 1983. He started his letter by telling me to find a decent taekwondo school and get back to training as soon as I can. His letter congratulated me for trusting the Lord, and he encouraged me to get into the word of God. He wrote, "The closer you get to God, the more you will understand." He added this admonition: "A farmer loses his distinction as a farmer if he does not cultivate and plant seeds in his garden. A Christian loses his distinction if he does not cultivate and plant seeds in the hearts of unbelievers and if he does not continue to lead the lifestyle that is acceptable to God. It is not easy to be a Christian." He concluded by wishing me the very best of happiness and joy in my new life and welcomed me into the family of God. Despite my short time with Senior Grand Master Sell, he'd become a hero to me.

The practice of taekwondo always grounds me and brings me back to feeling like I've accomplished something.

Finish what you begin. That thought reverberates in my brain. *Here's another shot at being part of something that matters and competing at a sport I love.* With the intense physical and mental demands of being a soldier, I know that the vigor of my training promises to double my workload if I elect to add athlete to my identity as a warrior for my country. I never enter into any commitment lightly.

Late that afternoon, I find SPC Pedro Laboy and SGT Raphael Medina—both from Puerto Rico—and a special ops guy and a sergeant training together under the auspices of the Morale, Welfare, and Recreation area of the post. I meet them for the first time and Laboy explains the goal: to medal at the state tournament a few months away, so that we could become the first official US Army team at the nationals.

A lot of soldiers studied taekwondo before us, and the Navy and Air Force had fielded official teams, but not the Army.

That tells me everything I need to know. This gentle giant of a man isn't afraid to dream big. I commit right away because I see a chance to show others what I am capable of.

We train daily before sunup and after sundown. We fight each other and work on technique. But what we are doing is under the radar, since the US Army doesn't recognize any official teams in taekwondo as a supported sport yet. Some of the officers on the base treat us like we are trying to use this pursuit to get out of regular duties. We all make sure to fulfill our obligations and keep training time strictly to off-hours.

Sports keep soldiers in top physical condition, but to be one of the best in your sport takes time and tremendous discipline. The task of balancing being a soldier and an athlete simultaneously is not an easy one. You must get up early in the morning and get ready for physical training, maintain your job skills, participate in field-training exercises, and perform any additional task that lies ahead. Soldiers are soldiers twenty-four hours a day, seven days a week. To wear the title of soldier-athlete means doubling down in every area and sacrificing what little personal and family time you have.

Laboy acts as our coach since he got some training when he was stationed in South Korea, and has represented Puerto Rico in international competitions. We do demonstrations, and Laboy teaches classes to try and drum up support for a sport that still isn't well known.

At the state championships with Medina (bantamweight), Laboy (heavyweight), and me (lightweight and featherweight), all take the gold in our respective weight classes.

A week after the local newspaper does a big write-up on our small team, our Commanding Officer calls us in for a meeting. He

tells us that the Moral, Welfare, and Recreation program has agreed to fund us in our pursuits, and we are allowed to be on orders to travel and fight. We are now the pioneer team who has official permission to wear the black and gold and represent the US Army in the nationals.

Mark as a member of the inaugural US Army taekwondo team

(photo credit: Pedro Laboy)

We contain ourselves until we get outside, and then we break loose, yelling and hugging each other. These guys have quickly become family to me even though we couldn't be more different.

CHAPTER TEN

BREAKING THROUGH

You may encounter many defeats, but you must not be defeated. In fact, it may be necessary to encounter the defeats, so you can know who you are, what you can rise from, how you can still come out of it.

—Maya Angelou

Over the next months, we redouble our efforts. We are determined to represent Fort Bragg well. Now that we officially have the thumbs up from our Company Commanders, we are allowed to practice taekwondo during the hours of 0500–0630 and 1300–1630, and our superior officers no longer give us a hard time.

We work hard many hours after a long, grueling day, sometimes coming back from jumps and then still working out. We suit up, practice speed drills, do calisthenics, and stretch with a cooldown. We move to Callahan Gym, where Buster Douglas is training for his heavyweight fights. We run tournaments at Fort Bragg and do demonstrations for Moral, Welfare, and Recreation. We also visit high schools and do demonstrations to assist recruiters.

For our first national tournament, Pedro works with the Fort Bragg's sports office. We get sponsored out of the leftover budget from the boxing team. Unlike most official military teams, we still don't have an official coach. Laboy serves in that role since he is on the national team for Puerto Rico.

Our black T-shirts emblazoned with US Army in big, gold letters across the back and our names on the front arrive. What we've accomplished starts to sink in. We are the pioneer Army team in this sport.

On June 7, 1985, we fly to Hartford, Connecticut, to compete in the eleventh United States Taekwondo Union (USTU) Championships, representing the US Army for the first time.

My heart is thumping against my chest as we enter the convention center. I settle down after I easily trump my first opponent.

For my second bout, I am matched against last year's champion in the weight class. I am fast; I kick hard and I give it my all.

***

When our bout is over, the five judges take a long, long time deliberating over their decision. In the end, the referee walks over to my opponent and raises his right hand as the judge's pick for the winner. In my heart I know I beat him, but in this sport, like all sports, politics come into play. The only thing that makes me feel a little better is the fact that he goes on to take the gold that day.

Laboy and Medina get the same results. None of us medal that year at the nationals. Nobody likes to lose, but we know we put in a good showing for the black and gold, and we head back to the base, confident that we can hold our heads high.

We continue to train hard on a daily basis. The following year we have the support of the Department of the Army's Sports Office based in Virginia. On April 5,1986, our team of four—Laboy, Medina, SGT Leo Oledan (flyweight) and me—travels to Dayton, Ohio, to compete in the twelfth United States Taekwondo Union Championships in Dayton, Ohio. Again, none of us medal.

We meet fellow Army soldier-athlete Master Sgt. Bruce Harris. He pulls us aside and says, "You know, the Olympic Committee selected taekwondo as the official demonstration sport for the 1988 Olympic Games in Seoul, Korea."

We are all electrified by his words. He believes in us.

***

Sometimes when we take a hard look at ourselves, we don't like what we see. We don't want to see the truth. Good coaches and mentors know how to expose our weaknesses, and they'll help you conquer them. Being able to turn your weaknesses into strengths is often the difference between winning and losing.

In taekwondo, it was just me on my own at times when I couldn't afford a coach or take classes. I had to look inside, and I had to get the mindset. I had to psych up and give myself the talk: *I'm going to beat this guy. I'm going to show him right away that I'm a pursuer. I'm going to be aggressive. I'm going to take the fight to him, and I'm also going to be a good defensive fighter.* There were times I got beat up, but that was okay because that's part of growing.

You are not going to win all the time. But if you can find mentors and learn from them, you have a much stronger chance of success at something than you do trying to go it alone. Sure, you've got to put in the time. You've got to put in the effort. You've got to put in the sweat. You've got to fight through injuries and stay on top of your game. You've got to give it to get it.

You also don't always get the mentoring you want. As a preteen and teenager, I wanted the money to be able to go take more classes and didn't have it. I wanted my little brother, who had become a national champion placing second in the nation in our sport, to go to the US Olympic training camp in Colorado Springs where he could get top coaching, but our family didn't have the money. Those experiences and overcoming what we can't have and doing the best that we can anyway bring a victory of its own.

***

One morning we file into the auditorium to see a motivational speaker. To my surprise, Senior Grand Master Sell stands on the stage. I learn that he is contracted with the Department of Defense to visit installations around the world and give demonstrations to service members to motivate them. An ordained minister, Senior Grand Master Sell preaches hope and shows what taekwondo requires of the mind, body, and spirit.

I am overwhelmed with emotion. I have been training for the nationals with the pioneer team at Fort Bragg, and many years have passed since I had seen him. I realize I had followed his advice to get stronger spiritually and to continue my taekwondo training. All I had was the letter he wrote me and my memories of doing demonstrations with him in Florida. He used to cut watermelons on my stomach with a samurai sword.

We enter the old auditorium, and I see five large stacks of bricks set up for breaking on the wooden stage. Some of my buddies know I am a fighter and have a black belt. The chaplain knows, too. After Senior Grand Master Sell smashes a couple of the stacks with his bare hands, there was one large stack left in the middle of the stage. Our chaplain belts out, "Where is Specialist Green? He is a black belt, and he can break those bricks!"

My buddies around me start chanting. Soon the entire room is egging me on to go up on stage and break those bricks.

I hesitate, because I haven't broken bricks since my time with the Senior Grand Master. I do not want to be the laughing stock of the 82nd Airborne for not breaking them if I try and fail.

Senior Grand Master Sell motions me up on stage. At that point, there is no turning back. The group around me cheers when I stand up and walk to the center of the stage in my uniform and shined jump boots. I survey the stack of bricks to ensure they are straight and set up properly. I have never attempted to break that many before, so I am nervous. A small cloth is folded on top of the stack, but I never like anything on top the bricks, so I toss it to the ground. The crowd cheers.

I line up on the bricks. The moment of truth has come. I let out a taekwondo yell and drive through the entire stack, sending them crashing to the wood stage floor with a huge booming sound. The support bricks fell as well, so only a big pile of rubble remained.

Everybody goes wild. I cannot hear myself think in that auditorium.

Senior Grand Master Sell gives me a smile of acceptance and nods his approval.

I love being in his presence. Not only is he physically strong, but more importantly, he possesses a great strength of character and is a mentor to me. He is one of the men who saved me. He told me once that he couldn't be my friend. When he saw the expression on my face, he said, "I have to be your instructor, and I can't be both."

Mark after his victory at his first fight at the national championships in 1985

(photo credit: Pedro Laboy)

CHAPTER ELEVEN

THE FRENCH CONNECTION

*The brave may not live forever, but the cautious do not live
at all.*

—Unknown

As a warrior athlete on Fort Bragg, I meet my next mentor: Lieutenant Colonel Robert Flowers (LTC Flowers), my battalion commander for the 82nd Airborne. The son of a career military man who'd lived all over the world, he is the best leader I have ever served with to this point. He keeps the morale high by being creative in keeping us fit to fight. For an adrenaline junkie like me, that keeps me going. Maybe his sense of fun had something to do with being the father of five boys.

One time we go for a battalion run, and in the middle of the exercise out of nowhere, a UH-1H helicopter lands right in the middle of us. Soldiers get out and do a perimeter around it like they are protecting the chopper. The shock factor he incorporates into our morning physical fitness while we are running through the pine trees of the back acres of Fort Bragg is what makes it fun. When a helicopter shows up and the chop of the air from the blades makes the sound it does, it motivates people.

Later during that same run, we stop again, and aerobics instructors in Lycra leotards pop out from behind trees, start blasting music, and take our battalion of engineers through routines. How often can you say that you have done aerobics in the woods of Fort Bragg with music blaring in those conditions? And they are tough exercises, too.

With the pressures of being ready to deploy anywhere in the world in a matter of hours, LTC Flowers knows that morale is important.

LTC Flowers always finds some way to show us that we are the best. Positivity and praise were in short supply for me growing up. The more he praises us and expects great things from our battalion, the more I find myself fighting even harder to live up to his confidence in us.

He is practical, too. Because as engineers in the Army, we often had to put pickets in the ground to put up wire, he conjures up something he calls the picket run. The pickets are heavy, about six feet long and U-shaped with sharp edges. You have to watch your hands when you're running with them. We go out for a four-mile run holding these pickets out in front of us like they are rifles. It sounds like a crazy thing to do, but these pickets are one of the tools of our trade. Running with them is just another way to get our minds off the exercise and have fun doing it.

I take an interest in the Soldier of the Month competition, which I win two times that year for my company. You have to have an excellent uniform and answer board questions after reporting to a panel of top noncommissioned officers. You have to be confident

Private First Class Mark Green, paratrooper in 82nd Airborne, 1984

and know your stuff in many different military subjects. I am chosen to compete for the Soldier of the Year in the battalion, which is a combat unit of about five hundred to eight hundred soldiers.

The competition for that is even tougher, because you have to do a physical fitness test, do the actual skills, and also do the board portion. I win it for the battalion under LTC Flowers. To my surprise, because I win Soldier of the Year, I get added to an exchange with foreign paratroopers. I am excited when I find out I got onto the list. My life is getting better. A trip to France in an exchange program with the French Army is something all paratroopers want because you can wear foreign jump wings on your Class A uniform.

I've barely seen any of the United States, much less been out of the country. France sends one hundred paratroopers to the US, and I am one of one hundred paratroopers selected to go to Montabon, France.

I get my first surprise shortly after we arrive at this small village in the northwest of France. American paratroopers are used to eating a big breakfast: pancakes, bacon, eggs, fruit, milk, juice, toast, and cereal.

We arrive jet-lagged just in time for breakfast, and we are one hungry bunch. We go to breakfast and are served steaming cups of cocoa and coffee and a piece of hard bread. That's it. *Whoa, this is different.*

Lunch brings the second surprise of the day when wine flows generously. Thankfully, the food is generous portions at this meal, which also happens at a much more leisurely pace than we are accustomed to. US paratroopers don't normally drink during the day—and especially not before we go jump out of an airplane, and especially one that is not the same type of airplane you're familiar with, along with a parachute different than what you typically use.

Most days, we'd do our jumps, and then our French hosts, who have a mixture of commandos on the team, would say, "Let's go grab a cocktail."

We did our share of drinking at night, but this was a whole different culture. We hung out with them in the evenings exchanging military patches and sharing stories. In the first week, the commandos set up an obstacle course across a river and up the side of a mountain cliff. It had to have taken them time, because these were complex obstacles. In constructing the course, they used cannons to shoot nets up the side of the mountain and then fastened them over big boulders, ran zipline cables over the river, and created barriers out of enormous logs. It was built to challenge us, and I think as a welcome-to-our-world kind of introduction. The French prove to be some tough guys.

On the final night, we do exchanges with patches and pins. The one item that means the most to me is presented to me at the Foreign Jump Wing presentation to those of us who completed the training. We all get our own set of Foreign Jump Wings. On the back, the pin has a number that no one else can ever be given. That is not done in the US.

I am top fit. I am top trained. In that moment, I'm happy again, because I own my own life. I own my decisions.

CHAPTER TWELVE

NO FAIRY-TALE ENDING

The man who can drive himself further once the effort gets painful is the man who will win.

—Roger Bannister

As an E-4, I don't have a lot of money, but I am getting a regular paycheck. I live off post, because there aren't enough rooms for everyone on base. I like the extra freedom of having my own place. Sometimes I run a little short and have to go to the pawnshop. But I make the best of it.

I sell my truck and buy a Jeep, a little CJ-5. I am proud of my Jeep, and I keep it shined. I own something tangible that I can show for my three years in the Army.

One holiday weekend, I jump in my Jeep and head down with some friends to Myrtle Beach, South Carolina. I'm a paratrooper, and I feel good. The movie *Top Gun* has just come out, and it's a great story about the military and love.

We plan to stay in the state park, but the camping sites are already full, so we stay in the overflow area of the park. The heat is sweltering that weekend, so we spend all our time swimming in the ocean and hanging out on the beach.

I notice this blonde girl, who is talkative and bubbly. I'd never encountered a bubbly girl like her. She tells me she goes to North Carolina State, and her dad works for IBM. By the end of the weekend, we hit it off, and I ask if I can call her.

We start dating. Every weekend that I can, I make the drive from Fort Bragg to spend time with her at NC State. I slow down my taekwondo training and start spending lots of time with her.

I keep training, and she comes to watch me fight in the state championships. As time goes by, we get serious. Taekwondo starts to take a back seat to the girl.

I finish out my tour with the 82nd Airborne, and I decide to leave Fort Bragg. After two years of being on the US Army team and fighting in a total of four nationals without medaling—counting my two times at the nationals as a teen—I decide I may not have what it takes to make it all the way to the Olympics anyway.

After all, in the four national championships I've fought in, I've never placed higher than the silver, and that was when I was a high school junior long ago. Laboy and Medina keep up the pace and get approved by the Department of Defense to represent the Army at the Pan American Games.

I have this nagging feeling that I am missing out, but after three years of balancing the dedication required to be both a high-level athlete and a soldier in the Airborne, I decide I want to pursue the girl. My mind is made up.

She invites me home to New York for Thanksgiving with her family. I get authorized leave and accompany her home.

While I am there my heart says, *You should ask her to marry you. This is your second chance at love.*

I ask her dad if he'll take a walk with me, and this time I ask for her hand in marriage. He gives us his blessing.

I am on top of the world with a beautiful girl. Again I am granted leave. I pick up my five-year-old daughter in Arkansas from my first marriage so she can attend our outdoor wedding in Minnesota. The wedding is very small, but it feels like a fairy tale to me. Her family welcomes me with open arms. By the end of the night, all I can think is *Things are going to be all right.*

We begin our marriage by agreeing to go to college first and get settled before having a family. Little do I know she is already pregnant when she walks down the aisle.

When she breaks the news a few weeks after we have tied the knot, she informs me that she wants to move to be with her family. I let my Company Commander know that I am not reenlisting and will be leaving Fort Bragg.

The clock is ticking on my ninety-day out, which means I am required to leave the service ninety days before my four years is up. I am sweating, worrying how I'm going to pay for a new baby.

Lieutenant Colonel Flowers steps in and allows us to extend for medical reasons to pay for the baby. That is a huge burden off my shoulders. Because I am active-duty military, our daughter is born at Fort Bragg. Once again, I owe a debt of gratitude to that man, who looked at our situation with compassion. Her pregnancy is almost full term when it is time to leave, but he arranges for us to stay.

When I leave the service, I go from being a paratrooper with regular money coming in to no money. I am floundering. I try working a night shift as a machinist. But my boss is working me twelve-hour shifts. I am falling asleep at the wheel on the forty-five-minute drive home every morning. Soon she is pregnant again, and our son is born. I work as a machinist and at a series of jobs building houses. Failure piles on top of failure. I am not fulfilling my obligation as a father or husband. We fight often.

At this point, I haven't learned to keep my temper under control. I start to feel like the loser she often tells me I am. Before long, our family of four moves in with her mom and dad. Once her father dies unexpectedly, her frustration with me hits the boiling point.

I decide that I am going to be a real estate broker. I take the real estate exam and pass. *Maybe she'll be proud of me.*

Then five years and two kids into the marriage, I see her at the park one day, laughing and talking with one of the residents from the hospital where she works. When I confront her, she says, "Our marriage is over. I'm going to marry a doctor."

I am in complete shock, because I realize that she's thinking divorce. Next thing I know she somehow connects with a resident in Italy. She takes our children with her and moves there to be with him. Before she leaves, she turns our friends against me and files false claims that I do not deserve. I am lonely, desperate to see my little daughter and son with no idea of whether that will ever happen again.

I have no problem accepting responsibility for anything I have done, but I will never accept responsibility for something I have not done. I spin into depression just as I've gotten my real estate license and started a new business as a broker.

While I am working as a salesperson in real estate and in the midst of the divorce, my manager tells me, "You have to learn to turn the tape off."

At first, I do not know what he is saying. Later I realize that he is warning me that our minds rerun bad things over and over like a broken record. You somehow have to halt your negative thoughts, or you'll spin out of control.

The divorce drains what little money I have, and I am forced to file bankruptcy. I beat myself up for starting a real estate business in the middle of this mess. I don't have enough money to keep our house. We sell it, and she gets the proceeds.

I couch surf at a friend's. Now I can't afford insurance for my car or rent money. I am basically homeless, depressed, and isolated, and I feel useless.

Then I get a listing for my brokerage for this Christian family's property. I ask, "Can I lease this property from you, and when I sell it, I'll pay what I owe?"

They agree to the deal. In my gut, I know it's a stupid deal, because it's a huge conflict of interest. I'm living in the house, trying to sell it, and my sign is in the front yard.

I feel so detached, I lock myself in that house and do not come out for days. I am so out of it that they turn the electricity off for me not paying the bill and the little food I have spoils in the refrigerator. I can't eat, I can't sleep, and I feel completely defeated. I am in shock that I could be treated the way I have been.

In the end, I lose the listing and owe the family the money I'd promised. They turn me in for the debt, and I lose my real estate license. Now on top of what I am already dealing with, I have no job either, except for trying but failing to be a realtor and being a weekend warrior E-4 in the National Guard.

I start to wonder how many times I'm going to have to start over.

As part of my job, I visit the landlord of the apartments my ex lived in. I learn that she and the kids are coming back to the United States. When she returns to Minnesota after ten months and the Italian dumping her, she has softened a little. She tells me I can see the kids anytime.

I am ecstatic. That's the only bright moment I've had in a long time. I have missed my kids so much.

Now I am constantly behind on my child support thanks to making yet another bad choice. I remember a saying I'd heard along the way: "When there's no money in the front door, love's out the back." Truer words were never spoken in our case.

Something is burning in the back of my mind. In our heated exchanges over the months prior to our divorce, she often told me, "You will never be an officer in the Army. You can't hold a job. You don't even have a college degree, and you're such a loser there's no way you'll ever finish that."

Her words stung and brought back what my uncle always told me: "You'll never make anything of yourself. You're just trailer trash."

Now here a woman I once loved was standing before me, hurling those same words at me. I felt less than a man. She crushed any confidence I have ever had in myself.

I feel like I've let her win. After a heart-to-heart discussion with a National Guard chaplain, something clicks. Her furious disdain awakens my warrior spirit and my determination to do something great. *I need to show you that I can do things you have no idea I can do.*

Despite my ongoing fight with depression and my newfound habit of trying to drown my sorrows, I sign up for college courses, using the National Guard money and the GI Bill. I start working out again as a stress reliever and to remind myself that I've been an elite athlete who knows how to win. I make so-so grades, but still, it's a start toward a new life.

CHAPTER THIRTEEN

AN OFFICER AND A GENTLEMAN

Failure is not an option.
—Gene Kranz

When I was three years old, a picture was taken on July 25, 1965, of me and my sister on the porch of our Missouri home. We are standing with my dad's Second Lieutenant officer hats on. I have on the dress green hat, and my sister has the steel pot on and is trying to hold it down on her head. I am standing with my arms at parade rest.

Mark with sister Kelly in their dad's military hats

I keep that picture on my desk to remind me that my destiny as a soldier was imprinted in my mind early in life. Although my father did not make it a career, the first eight years of my life were immersed in the Army. When he'd go plan for training, my dad, an engineer captain in the Missouri National Guard, would take me with him to the Jefferson Barracks. The halls smelled like cigars.

I used to stand in front of that house in Arnold and salute as I watched the Army convoys drive by. I was hooked.

My father's love of alcohol eventually got him in trouble, and at ten years of service, he left the National Guard.

I had joined the Army because I needed a skill, I needed money, and I needed the education I blew off.

Now I have heavy responsibilities. When I get challenged and slapped in the face with failure, the warrior awakens within. I realize I've got options. I am determined not to follow in my father's footsteps. *A winner is just a loser who gets up one more time*, I remind myself.

When I joined the Army, I took the service's battery of tests. It had been three years since I left high school. I had not cracked a math book or English book during that time, and had lost most all of the algebra and other English skills I had learned.

My test scores coming into the Army allowed me to pick the job I wanted, but my general technical score was not quite high enough to allow me to pursue becoming an officer.

I start working on my college degree at Rochester Community College. I still have the desire to become an officer, but I know I must to go back and study and retake the test. I retake it and receive way above the score I need to apply.

I am required to get waivers because I will be almost thirty-three years old by the time I graduate if I successfully complete Officer Candidate School (OCS).

The Minnesota Military Academy Officer Candidate School program is located in Camp Ripley, Minnesota. Next door they train Minnesota state troopers. The program lasts from sixteen to eighteen months. It also means that I have a long drive back and forth each weekend to attend.

Our class starts with somewhere between forty-five and sixty candidates. It is physically and mentally challenging. The candidates in Class 38 are definitely tested. We lose some of our officer candidates due to land navigation, a failed test, or injuries they experience outside of training. Some simply cannot handle the pressure of it all and resign.

***

One night after school, I'm out having a beer at a place called Ed's Attic—our town of Rochester's version of the *Cheers* bar—with friends, who introduce me to a whole other group of friends.

I am now thirty-two years old, an E-4 specialist in an infantry company of the Army National Guard. I am feeling on top of the world because I am close to finishing my officer's training. I have been working out a lot and am healthy. I've already been through four years of the Army, a couple years in the Reserves, and two marriages.

The last thing I am looking for is another relationship. I just want to keep my head down and get my life back on track.

Then through the crowd, I see this this brown-haired, brown-eyed, milky-skinned, beautiful, beautiful woman leaning up against the wall on the backside of the bar.

I stop dead in my tracks. Turns out that she is with the group of friends that my group is connected with. I introduce myself, and one of my woman pals yanks up my shirt and says, "Oh, look at these abs."

Everybody laughs and we're having a good time, but it's crowded and people are drinking. I'm on my way to the bathroom when this guy purposely knocks into me with his shoulder. I bow up and we come close to blows. She happens to be standing right there.

So later that night after I leave the bar, I call the number she'd scrawled on a scrap of paper. I want to apologize because I feel bad for that being her last impression of me—a hothead, ready to fight.

"Hello?"

"It's Mark. I want to apologize for that thing that happened in the hallway," I say.

She laughs and then says, "Well, at least you know now that the number is good."

I can't help but smile and say, "I'll call you tomorrow. Good night."

***

In the end, Class 38 has to learn to work together to get things done. We become a tight squad—perhaps one of the tightest teams in the academy's history—because we are pushed the hardest. The percentage of graduates prior to our class are much higher. The

Colonel in charge of the program tells the Captain who pushes everyone so hard to back off because it is affecting the program in a negative way.

In spite of my fears, Denise and I start dating. She's a nurse and understands how important it is for me to study hard almost every night. She patiently helps me with my studies.

I receive the second-highest award in the class for leadership for Class 38. *Second in the class.* We call ourselves the "8 from 38," because only eight of us are left standing after the two years of grueling curriculum and physical challenges.

Mindset means being ready for anything. For me, the process of learning how to be a leader is a rewarding task. I write the Governor of Minnesota about our class's accomplishment and receive a letter commending us in return.

The Army uses West Point, the Reserve Officers' Training Corps, and Officer Candidate School to prepare young leaders for their assignments as officers in the US Army. The officers I graduate with have the mettle to get through anything. I am confident of this because I've seen them become flexible, adaptable, and equipped to deal with hundreds of stressful situations over the time we were together.

I am on top of the world. I have stepped out of the old attitudes and shed my old, limiting beliefs. A sense of pride fills my entire being. It seems a lifetime ago since that frigid day in New Jersey on the drill field, when I shivered against the cold, wondering what my future held.

CHAPTER FOURTEEN

THIRD TIME'S THE CHARM

The greatest explorer on this earth never takes voyages as long as those of the man who descends to the depth of his heart.

—Julien Green

I start to think I've finally found the right woman. Denise comes from a hardworking farm family whose ancestors immigrated from Italy. She's honest, down-to-earth, and as a nurse, she's compassionate. There's no pretense about her.

After we are together a while, we decide to take a camping and canoeing trip in the boundary waters up by Canada. To explore the boundary waters, you have to go through the state-park system and apply for a permit. Everything you take into the area, you have to bring back out.

It's God's country, so much like heaven that it takes your breath away—the wildlife, the fish, and the waters where you can see forty feet to the bottom. You scarcely see a soul beyond the moose, deer, and bear that roam the territory. I've never seen a more pristine place in all my time spent outdoors.

We go up with two other couples: my best friend and his girlfriend, and her cousin and her husband. We bring three canoes, and we all carry in our own water and our own packs. The first day we hike in seven miles, but that was a little too far. We are all so tired by the time we carry the canoes and our gear back to camp that we lie down and fall asleep.

Part of the fun is jumping from lake to lake and seeing the waterfalls that are between some of them, because of the gradient change from glaciers in Minnesota centuries ago. But as you come to the end of the lake where you need to take your canoe out, that waterfall can be treacherous because of the water's swiftness, its turbulence, and the rocks. You have to time it just right to get out and pull your canoe, gather your gear, and then go onto the next lake.

On the second day, I wait a little too long to get out of the canoe and pull it to the side. With Denise still inside, I jump out and grab the canoe, but the water starts pushing it sideways. Next thing I know, I'm upstream from the canoe with my hands in the center. Denise is in the back of the canoe, looking me right in the eyes and shouting, "Don't you let go. Don't you let go."

I am sweating and struggling against the current that threatens to drag her over the falls. I am scared to death because I am certain she'll be hurt or worse if I let go. I am strong, but holding on is taking everything I've got and then some.

I make myself think of my taekwondo training—all those times when I thought I had nothing left and I dug deep and found a little more. Just as I feel the water ripping at my grip, I find something inside and give it everything I have. I turn the tip of that canoe upstream and get her safely out.

A wave of relief sweeps over me, and I mop the sweat pouring off my brow. "Oh my God, I cannot believe that just happened," I say, collapsing beside her on the bank, once I got the canoe turned over and clear of the rapids.

"I'm just glad you didn't let go," Denise says. "I probably wouldn't have forgiven you for that one."

The rest of the trip is uneventful but loads of fun—except for the blackflies that bite and pester you that time of year. All day long we canoe, fish and cook our own food, and savor the fresh air.

Two days in, though, one of the women pipes up and says, "I can't do this." I remember the guys who washed out of the 82nd.

The problem is that we only brought two compasses among the three couples. Having been in the Army, I know how to use my compass. I also know that the other one is off. This woman throws a fit and insists that they are leaving, so I take my compass and chart their route back. I give them my compass and an extra map for their trip. She doesn't consider that we could get lost or run into a bear. All she is thinking about is herself.

But we see them off. Then it's just my best buddy and his girlfriend, and Denise and me. Perfect. We fix a lunch on the shore of a pristine lake, then spend the afternoon laughing and paddling around in the water. The last day it pours rain. We are soaking wet, fighting the wind and the lightning. We get lost for a few minutes because it's raining so hard we can't see where we are going.

That's when I know that I've finally lucked into the woman of my dreams. She doesn't cry or complain the whole trip. She is tough and strong.

We go back to Rochester. I'm in school, and I'm looking for jobs. She's got three jobs. I've got one job, and that one is kind of iffy, selling water filters and just doing whatever I can find to get by.

Sometimes Denise comes with me when I see my kids. We take them to the park, or I take them fishing. As they get older, I pick them up and drop them off at a Dairy Queen between our town and where they live. Our visits become more and more infrequent—not from my side—but because my ex always has a reason why they can't come.

***

One day on the way to Denise's folks' house, we pass an old, rundown farmhouse in the middle of several acres. "Honey, who lives there?" I ask.

"Oh, it's our neighbor's farm."

I go over to the neighbor's farm the next day and knock on the door. "I'm looking for a job up here," I say. "Would you be interested in giving me a reduced rent to fix up the place down the street and rent it from you?"

He rubs his chin and adjusts his greasy ball cap, and says, "Well, why don't you go down and look at it to be sure you want to take it on?"

I make a list of all the things that need to be done: plumbing, new toilets, work on the well, the grass cut, and lots of painting. The outbuildings are falling down, but the house is next door to

Denise's parents, and it has hardwood floors. We make an agreement that I'll pay a nominal amount and fix up the place.

I love this beautiful setting out in the Minnesota countryside. I plant a garden on the eight acres. I park my little boat out there and fish as often as I can. I plant the tomato row right next to the overgrown lawn, so I can snag a fresh tomato off the vine while I'm driving the tractor and cutting the grass.

***

Finally, the day comes for our wedding. All I can think is that this makes the third time I've watched a woman walk down the aisle. It's either third time's the charm, or three strikes and you're out. My kids do not attend that day because they've just gotten back from Italy, and I feel like it's too much to ask. Later, I realize that I should have had them there regardless.

I am marrying my best friend in this tiny Lutheran church right in downtown Rochester. She's ten years younger than me, and I know she's not after my money, because I don't have any.

My best man flies up in a snowstorm. Nobody else is on my side of the church, because after all, it's my third time around.

We are standing next to each other as I watch Denise come down the aisle on her father's arm. She's beaming and looks more beautiful than I've ever seen her.

We are saying our vows and the pastor asks me, "Do you take this woman to be your lawfully wedded wife?"

I freeze. I'm not sure if I am too full of emotion or it's because I know that if I say these words again and don't back them up 100 percent, I'm a crazy man, a fool, an idiot. *Why would you do this again? Why would you put yourself through so much pain?* All those thoughts are racing through my brain. There is a long pause after he asks me the question.

Finally, my best man reaches over and taps me on the shoulder. I take a deep breath and say, "I do."

CHAPTER FIFTEEN

A MIRACLE

Out of difficulties grow miracles.
—Jean de la Bruyere

I am still in the Army Reserves, and I apply for a unit-administrator job that pays much more than what I was making as a realtor. My new job requires some travel, and I don't like the idea of leaving my wife alone way out in the country.

We need some security because people are breaking into houses. My buddy's American Kennel Club (AKC) Rottweiler sires some puppies, and I buy one from him for protection.

Growing up we always had dogs around, but I didn't pay much attention to them because most of them were strays who were too shy to come around us.

Once we get Hercules, nobody ever comes knocking on our door unless they are invited and we are at home.

I am unprepared for what happens next. This puppy steals my heart. I name him Hercules. He is happy and loving, eager to learn, and fiercely loyal. I leave him off the leash because I want him to patrol the entire property.

Hercules goes everywhere with me. I take a picture of him wearing one of my T-shirts with a photo of him wearing sunglasses. I love Hercules.

My brother Dale had enlisted in the Navy. One night he was riding on the back of a motorcycle and had a bad wreck and suffered a traumatic brain injury. After the accident, he gets in some trouble and is forced out of the military. We invite him to stay with us while he gets his life sorted out.

When I go to Texas for some Army training, I explain my routine with Hercules to my brother. "When you go to the mailbox, Hercules will follow you to the end of the driveway," I say. "When you get to the end, you have to stop and look at him and tell him to sit. He will stay there until you walk across the road and walk back to him. If you don't turn around and tell him to stay, he could get hit by a car."

"Okay, I got it," he says. "I'm good. No worries."

"I know it's just a two-lane county road, but the grain trucks and other folks speed out here in the country."

I have been gone for a day or so to coordinate for some Army training in Fort Bliss, Texas, near El Paso, when I get the news. My brother forgot to turn around. Hercules followed him into the road. My dog was hit and killed instantly.

I hang up the phone and cry—something I have hardly ever done in my entire life.

An impotent rage rises up inside of me. On a rational level, I know that my brother's brain injury is to blame, but on a primal level, I am so angry at him for his failure to listen.

I can't explain it, but my dog's death triggers a tsunami of emotions that I guess I'd buried a little deeper with every traumatic loss I'd suffered throughout my life. Sitting alone in that cheap motel room, wave after wave of grief washes over me.

Here I am so close to where my dad lives, but he has made it clear after my short visit to his home long ago that his new life only includes us when he wants it to. He expressed that to his new son in front of me, the number-seven child who has mostly been shielded from all six of us for his entire life. It's like all of us do not exist unless it works for him.

With that glum thought, the memories come crashing in, overwhelming me. My dad abandoning us so many years ago. The parade of men who came after Dad left. Not being allowed to graduate over a stupid prank gone awry on Senior Skip Day. Two failed marriages and the children I hardly ever get to see. Early teenage pregnancies of two of my sisters. The rape and attempted murder of a family member. The fighting, the drinking, the near-death experiences. Multiple divorces in our family. My brother Kayle's unsolved murder in St. Louis, Missouri. Because I was the unfortunate one who got called to clean up the crime scene in his apartment after the police concluded his murder investigation, the grisly aftermath of his death is seared into my brain. Trauma upon trauma.

And now, once again, something I love is gone, another small piece of my heart chipped away. If I am keeping score, the losses far outweigh the wins in my life at this point. *When is this going to stop? Am I ever going to catch a break?*

***

Shortly after that, my wife, Denise, tells me she wants to have a child. Her comment takes me by surprise. Before we married, we did discuss children but left it open ended since I had already fathered three.

I roll over and look into her beautiful eyes. We met when she was twenty-two years old. Now she is thirty. Denise comes from an Italian family, and she loves children.

My mind is racing. *I'm scraping to pay child support. She hardly ever asks for anything for herself. She works hard and supports me at every turn. How can I deny the heartfelt desire of the woman I love?*

"You really want a baby?" I ask.

"Yes, I want someone to call me Mommy," she replies. "I enjoy being a stepmom, but I want to hear 'Mommy, Mommy, Mommy' from our child."

I take a deep breath, hug her tightly, and whisper, "Okay."

Nothing ever comes easy. In my life, it seems that everything is always complicated. Months go by, and each month brings yet another disappointment.

After two and a half years pass with no positive news, we go to the Mayo Clinic to try to get answers about what the problem is. We decide to try the in vitro–fertilization (IVF) process.

The process itself is difficult. I give her intramuscular shots. I give samples to the doctor.

Each time we start with so much hope. We are willing life into existence. We want good news.

Then we go in and get the pregnancy test. Then we hear those words we don't want to hear: *I'm sorry, it didn't happen this time. . . . Sorry. . . . Sorry. . . . Sorry, not this time.*

We hear those words over and over and over again during the course of a year. I hold her when she cries. It hurts every single time we get the news.

It wears you down to nothing. Each month we mourn what might have been. We are so exhausted from the emotional roller coaster that we just want off. The strain on our relationship becomes almost unbearable. We wonder when that thread that binds our hearts together will fray.

This cycle of hope and grief went on for another two and a half years.

In the midst of all this angst, my ambitious, smart wife, who is a licensed practical nurse, starts school to become a full-fledged registered nurse.

Then one day I get a call. "You had some viable embryos, so we need to schedule for in vitro right away," the nurse says.

We go in, and then a few weeks later, I get the call. A voice on the other end of the line says, "Mr. Green, congratulations! It looks like your wife is pregnant." Denise had been given the bad news so many other times that she told the doctor to call me with the results of the next pregnancy test. She didn't want to hear the results from a stranger.

That night I bring flowers home with a card. She is curled up on the couch, studying. I can tell by the look that flickers across her face that she thinks the bouquet is the monthly sad consolation gift. Something she must acknowledge with a gratitude she doesn't really feel.

Then she opens the card.

I wrote, *Congratulations, Mommy, Mommy, Mommy.*

Swollen tears course down her checks.

"Really?" she asks, eyes glistening. "Is this true?"

***

Our son, Adam, is born at St. Mary's Hospital in Rochester, Minnesota, in 2001. Starting over with a new family, a new life.

When I see our son for the first time, I am overwhelmed with emotion.

I am forty years old. I've been abandoned and betrayed. I've been close to death. I've experienced the waters of baptism and the rebirth that it brings. I've been temporarily homeless. Each transition demands that I dig deep, that I discover the better man, who I am called to be.

Gazing at my tiny son and my wife's glowing face, I am determined to put the pain of my past in the rearview mirror and step bravely into the future.

I am confident about two things: I am resilient, and God always shows me the next steps. Stepping out of the past even when you have no proof that it's going to work out requires great faith.

CHAPTER SIXTEEN

ON THE MOVE

You are not judged by the height you have risen, but from the depth you have climbed.

—Frederick Douglass

When I complete the officer basic course in Fort Leonard Wood, Missouri, a Sergeant First Class says something that sticks with me: "Never bring today's dirt to tomorrow's formation."

He is not just talking about your boots and your gear. He means everything, including your attitude. Every day is a new day! Brush off the dirt, clean it off, and start over fresh.

After I receive my commission, we move multiple times to multiple states. When Denise agreed to marry me, she knew we were in for an adventure filled with uncertainty.

What I've learned by this point is that I can no longer afford to let the negative voices in my head hold me back from my dreams. I vow to myself that I am going to make progress in every area of my life no matter what. I start journaling my goals, affirmations, and my life mission statement.

I work on my higher education every time we get a chance. Denise matches the value I put on education, and as part of her journey, she goes to help children in Namibia, Africa, for a few weeks as part of her degree program from Augsburg University.

We have an agreement where we take turns giving each other the time and space to take courses and do whatever the next step is to better ourselves. We become a ready and resilient family and create a Green family motto: *Strength through adversity*.

Juggling full-time jobs, caring for our growing son, and full schedules at school for at least one of us and sometimes both of us simultaneously is challenging. But Denise is a trooper. She never complains. She matches me in drive and ambition.

I am doing my one weekend a month, and on those Friday nights that I have duty, I drive two-hundred-plus miles one way to the engineer battalion where I became a Second Lieutenant after I received my commission in July of 1994. I oversee a platoon of soldiers.

Our engineer unit is called out by the state of Minnesota to provide engineer support during a flood. We bring our drivers and dump trucks to haul sand. Our soldiers work around the clock filling sandbags, running generators, and monitoring and building the artificial dike that is holding back the floodwaters.

On the second day, my commander calls me aside and says, "I have an emergency and must leave. I'm putting you in charge."

As the highest-ranking officer on the scene, I understand, but the responsibility level went way up for me that very second. The weight of the situation going from supporting the effort to running the effort hangs over me.

Suddenly I am thrust into dealing with people on the dike, the corps of engineers, the media, the residents of the town, security, the Mayor and the Red Cross. We sleep in a local school but work around the clock in shifts.

The townspeople hold a town-hall meeting and ask tough questions. "Can you save our houses?" "How are you going to secure our homes?" I feel so much empathy. I remember what it was like when we lost our home when I was a teen to that industrial accident.

The Mayor and I agree that we will make no promises, but simply tell the worried folks that we will do our level best.

I have to step up and take charge, I tell myself. The river crests and then starts to recede. In the end, we save seven houses. I feel a huge sense of pride for not caving under the responsibility for our entire unit.

We are the classic Army family, taking orders and moving without question. Denise has always been independent and pursued her own goals. She makes enormous sacrifices in her own career. She moves around all these years and plugs in using her nursing skills wherever she can in whatever part of the US we are stationed—all without complaining.

We could allow all the constant change in our lives to stress us out and blow us apart. But early on, we agree to call each transition an adventure. In every new place we are assigned, we laugh about the adversity and crazy situations that sometimes arise. We celebrate every new rank and take school pictures of every first day of school for our son.

I finally catch a break and get picked up full time for the Army. At that point, I decide to get my master's degree and take classes at night. I sign up to study organizational management and communication at Concordia University, a Lutheran school with ten affiliated universities. We are stationed in Fort Snelling, Minnesota.

I've moved far from the way I viewed myself as a child and a teen when so many adults told me I was hopeless as a student. My shelves are filled with books on everything from self-help to leadership to inspiration.

I look forward to my classes and am confident that I belong in the relaxed cohort of professionals who have diverse, interesting backgrounds. All of us are nontraditional students—most from local corporations in the Minneapolis area. Almost without me noticing, something has happened that I never would have dreamed: I've become a lifelong learner.

Whenever I'm not working, I am studying. My wife quizzes me for my classes in the evenings. We critique each other's essays and schoolwork.

I get some great assignments as an officer: a command in Hawaii and a position as the planning chief for the Southwest United

States. Despite hard times and conflicts that arise from the frequent moves, the Army has been good for my family and for me.

My jobs are varied as an engineer. I am put in charge of platoons, handle many millions of dollars of infrastructure, and command a unit. With every job, my responsibilities increase, and thanks to good evaluations and results, the promotions keep coming.

As I leave command in Hawaii, I take a job as an Inspector General, one of the best jobs I have ever had in the Army. We are the eyes, ears, and conscience of the commanders. We are tasked to deal with issues from the commander, soldiers, family members, Department of the Army civilians, employees, retirees, and any other civilians needing any kind of assistance with an Army matter.

Inspector Generals are called upon to be honesty brokers and consummate fact finders, who use training, inspecting, assisting, and investigating as our primary tools. The inscription on the Inspector General crest is written in French: *Droit et Avant*. The motto's translation means "right and forward," which embodies the Inspector General philosophy of "First be right, then take action." Our instructors told us in school: First do your homework, and then go forward with the right answer.

Then our family faces one of our biggest challenges: I get my orders to deploy to Afghanistan. I'll be gone for a year.

CHAPTER SEVENTEEN

DEPLOYED

Never give in, never, never, never, never—in nothing great or small, large or petty—never give in except to convictions of honor and good sense. Never yield to force; never yield to the apparently overwhelming might of the enemy.

—Winston Churchill

Thanks to my tangled and difficult background and scrapping my way up the ranks from an enlisted soldier to an officer, I can relate to soldiers up and down the chain of command. Although I can attest to the fact that life is often unfair, I've developed a passion for upholding the truth and fighting injustice.

I am two years into my law-school studies at that point. During my yearlong deployment to Afghanistan in my role as an Inspector General, I am given responsibility for the southern half of the country, along the red desert from the borders of Pakistan to Iran. That means flying by Blackhawks, Chinooks, and contracted helicopters to check on the units and their morale, security, food service, ammo, fuel, mail delivery, housing, and safety throughout that region.

My days are spent listening to problems of every type and reporting up and down the chain of command as required.

Listening to a constant barrage of other people's troubles—particularly their relationship struggles—makes me miss my wife, Denise, and son all the more. We Skype sporadically every couple of weeks, so I am grateful to see their faces as often as I can. I think about the soldiers before me who had to rely on infrequent letters and mail drops as their sole means of connection.

I am lucky.

Still, my heart aches from the distance and the knowledge that there is much that I am missing at home. Adam, a tween, needs me. He and his mom have always been close, but given my own father's absence, I know how vital a father's role is in a boy's life. That knowledge, coupled with my constant exhaustion from the hypervigilance that comes from being in a war zone, weighs heavily on me.

Missing birthdays and holidays is hard for me. Seeing photos and images online of family and friends sometimes almost makes the hollow feeling in my chest grow worse.

Getting my law-school assignments and law reviews in on time presents a big challenge given the lack of bandwidth and lost connectivity on top of having to work on them in my few off-hours. Late one night in Kandahar, I've just attached the document for an important assignment and am just about to hit send on an important assignment, when the warning blared letting us know enemy rockets were incoming.

No way am I going to let a Soviet 122 mm rocket left over from the last war aimed in my general direction keep me from getting my assignment in on time that I have just finished and queued up in my email.

Instinctively, I duck under my bed, reach up until I can feel my laptop keyboard, and press the send button while secure, remaining in place before I head to the shelter.

About a month before I am slated to go home, my commanding officer calls me in to see him. "Congratulations, Major Green," he says, informing me that I am only one of three officers in my branch in the Army Reserve who have been preselected to attend the resident course of Command and General Staff College. This step is a prerequisite for Lieutenant Colonel.

I cannot wait to get on Skype with Denise and share the big news. I've already been counting the days until I'm home, and now I have something else to look forward to.

I am four weeks from the end of my deployment when I jump off the back gate a couple of feet off a C-130 aircraft after arriving at a forward operating base. The instant I hit the ground, I feel a searing pain in my right hip. I know something is seriously wrong. My adrenaline is pumping so high, I just keep moving.

From all those years making scores of jumps out of airplanes combined with my love of running and practicing taekwondo, my hips and knees have already taken a beating.

This time is different. I am so swollen, I have to ice everything and am unable to walk. I spend two days out of the fight, flat on my back. The medics give me intramuscular shots in both arms to take away some of the pain. I haven't felt this much pain since I got knocked out with a tire jack.

Since we are so close to our return date, the medical clinic gives me a prescription for the pain, and I gut it out.

CHAPTER EIGHTEEN

LEARNING TO WALK AGAIN

Patience and perseverance have a magical effect before which difficulties disappear and obstacles vanish.

—John Quincy Adams

I finish my post-mobilization at Fort Dix, New Jersey, the same installation at the time where I went to basic training more than twenty-seven years ago. Full circle. When I am released, I am greeted at the airport by Denise and Adam, who is holding a sign he made. It is almost ten o'clock at night, and the airport is quiet. I feel like I am in a movie. Everything feels surreal.

By the time I arrive home from active duty to Florida where my family is, I have lost twenty-three pounds. My right hip hurts so badly that I can hardly walk. Still, I am overjoyed at the sight of them. I've imagined this reunion for twelve long months.

All I want is to savor this reunion, get the keys to my car, go home and sink my teeth into a big, juicy cheeseburger, and pet my dog Moe. I want to get on with our life.

The next day we go see the orthopedic surgeon. After an x-ray and an examination, he explains that my hip had jammed so hard into the socket when I made that jump that it damaged the hip beyond repair.

"You need a full hip replacement," he says matter-of-factly. He adds that I'll likely never run again or compete at taekwondo. "The choice you have to make is pain-free fifties or pain-free seventies."

His words sting. *I am only forty-eight years old. This can't be right.* My thoughts go into rapid fire, leaving me dizzy.

As a high-energy guy with lots of energy to burn off, running has always been one of my releases, and taekwondo is part of who

I am. Plus, my semiannual physical fitness test at Command and General Staff College is only three months away.

I decide that I am going to do all I can to attend that resident course. If I can't pass the physical, I will not receive my next promotion to Lieutenant Colonel.

We are immediately thrust into survival mode as a family. I don't have time to process the emotional scars I've suffered from being in a war zone or from being away from my family for that year. All I can think about is what's happening to me physically. Denise takes charge of my rehabilitation and figures out a plan that gives me the best shot of rehabilitating in time to take the required physical fitness test.

I've been fortunate that other than stitches from my teen years as a scrapper, I've never been in the hospital and never had to have surgery. The surgery is grueling.

My discomfort is compounded by my fear that I'll fail to make that deadline. I have no idea what I'll do if I am out of the Army. I don't want to think about it, but at the same time, the specter of that possibility tortures me.

The first day after the surgery, a physical therapist comes into the room and moves my leg without warning me she was going to do it. The white-hot pain is instantly unbearable. In my morphine-addled state, I blurt out, "If you do that again without telling me first, I will not be responsible for the first ten seconds of what happens to you."

I realize in that moment, I am facing one of my biggest battles yet.

I have to learn to walk again. I am stressed to the max. In the beginning, no matter how much my mind commands my foot to move, my foot ignores the command. No amount of sheer grit and determination is enough. I've never faced anything like this before. I start to wonder if my desire to pass the alternate aerobic event that will determine if I continue my military career is a bridge too far.

Denise has mapped out my rehab schedule. As soon as I can stand, she has me out on the track at the local high school, walking every afternoon. She devotes her energies to my recovery and is with me every step of the way, nudging me, encouraging me, cajoling me, and making me laugh. But there are many gut-wrenching days when no laughing is going on. My tendency to get down on myself and easily frustrated is resurrected. I fall back in my old pattern of beating myself up for each failure rather than focusing on the small victories.

On top of trying to learn to walk again, I am trying to figure out how I fit into our family. Denise and Adam have formed an even tighter bond in my absence. My insecurity about whether I am needed and wanted flares. I feel like a burden due to my inability to get around in my own house.

I want to just pick up where we left off. One night I finally break down and tell Denise exactly how low I am feeling.

"I feel like an outsider in my own house," I say. "I'm a huge burden. I don't feel like either of you need me."

She stares at me for a minute, and then says, "While you were gone, Adam and I developed a routine. Sometimes it does feel like you are in the way, especially when you appear to be competing with the dog for who can be the laziest by lying around on the couch."

Hearing her voice out loud that indulging the moods of a broken-down paratrooper isn't part of her life plan gives me the kick that I need. "I don't mind helping you get well, but I do mind you throwing a pity party for yourself," she continues.

We start going to church regularly and find a local church we both feel good about. I'd been baptized years earlier when I was at basic training at Fort Dix, New Jersey, but once I got involved with the woman who became Wife Number Two, I had stopped attending church. More than two decades have passed, and I want to be a better man for my family.

***

One day during our morning walk at the track, my old temper flares up. I get so angry at what I perceive as my lack of progress that I hurl my cane down.

"Pick it up," Denise commands me. "You've got to keep going."

I lock gazes with her big, brown eyes for a moment. My head is pounding, and although it's early morning, I am already pouring sweat from the humidity of the hot Orlando summer. I can feel my pulse.

Finally, I pick up my cane, and we keep going.

When the day of my physical fitness test comes, I feel ready.

When I cross the finish line and realize I've passed, I let out a Missouri hoot for sheer joy. A sense of relief rushes over me. Once more I feel that high that comes from achieving something that you were told you couldn't do.

When it comes to my son Adam, I keep thinking everything would be back to normal if we could just go out for a long run together like we used to and blow off steam and frustration. But I can no longer run.

As I heal, I get involved in Boy Scouts, outdoor events, and baseball, and I help him set up his gamer crew with some kids in the neighborhood, so we can bond again. Once I actively mentor him, I begin to see the fruits of my efforts.

The year after my hip surgery, I tackle the Command and General Staff College Triathlon. Denise had signed up for it with a friend, and they are practicing for it. At first, I did not want to do it. Then something inside told me that I needed something to prove to myself that I could push past the trauma I wish no one has to go through.

I am the last one to finish that day because I am the only walker on the last leg of the triathlon. But I've proven something to myself: I never quit when it is important to me, and when it is, I am always moving forward.

CHAPTER NINETEEN

THE STORIES WE TELL OURSELVES

First comes thought; then organization of that thought, into ideas and plans; then transformation of those plans into reality. The beginning, as you will observe, is in your imagination.

—Napoleon Hill

In October of 2013 I finally graduate from William Taft Law School with a juris doctor. We've been assigned to the 63rd Regional Support Command and are renting on base in Mountainview, California. I am also promoted to Lieutenant Colonel in the same month.

Adam loves his school, and we develop a nice circle of friends and take long weekends up to the wine country. At a small cocktail party to celebrate my law degree, one of the guests asks, "What are you going to do with your degree?"

Without hesitation, I say, "Whatever I want to."

For the first time in my military career, I've begun to seriously think about what I want to do next in my life once I am out of the service. I know I won't practice law. I wanted my degree in the law solely to aid me as an entrepreneur. Though I'm not sure what I want to pursue yet, I know I want to be my own boss.

The day after the celebration, I feel oddly disquieted. Then it hits me. For the first time since I can remember, I don't have some big, crazy, impossible goal that I am striving for. I've been chasing after the next big thing my entire life.

Then I get a call from my brother Dale. "It's Mom," he says. "I need you here because she is really sick."

Dale has been living in Florida with Mom, who was widowed when her fourth husband committed suicide. Mom's fourth marriage appeared charmed until one day when he was involved in a traffic accident. The woman he hit told him that she was going to sue him for all he was worth. Afraid of leaving my mother with nothing, my stepfather in that instant made the decision to end his life.

Now she is facing another surgery from a second life-threatening disease, and my brother, who was injured in a motorcycle accident and suffered a brain injury, isn't equipped to handle the situation.

After discussing the situation with Denise, I put in a request for compassionate reassignment.

My request is denied, but only partially. Denise and Adam go back to Orlando. I am ordered to report to Fort Gillem, south of Atlanta, to work as a brigade engineer.

Denise's turn has come to pursue her next level of education, and she is about to start her clinicals to finish her studies to become a nurse practitioner when we get our new orders.

Now we have to set up two households and deal with separation again. I rent a small apartment site unseen near the base. I send a big deposit and am shocked when I see my new place. Nothing is as promised. Roaches skitter across the floor and gunshots ring out night after night. The door doesn't even lock properly. I sleep sitting up in an armchair, holding my gun and facing the door.

As soon as I have a few days off, I am on the road, making the seven-hour drive to Orlando. I make the trip multiple times just to see my family. With my wife in the middle of clinicals for her educational requirements, I am not about to ask her to move again when she is so close to completing her degree. I feel tremendous guilt because she is once again raising our teenage son alone and shouldering most of the burden of checking on Mom, who lives an hour and a half away in Tampa.

After about six months of living in two different states, I hit the wall emotionally. Alone in that crummy apartment in South Atlanta, I start to realize where my problems with never being able to let off the gas stem from. I've been in a state of hypervigilance ever since that night I went to sleep as an eight-year-old, dreaming of playing with my dad with my new baseball he'd given me for my birthday, and woke up to a life without Dad. I'd been stuck in that pattern ever sense.

***

Einstein called the definition of insanity doing the same thing over and over again yet expecting different results. I'm no Einstein, but I know I have to make some changes and fast if I want to get out of the deep, dark hole I am in.

I have to stop pretending I am superhuman and give myself permission to slow down every once in a while. That is a big shift in thinking for me.

Off and on, I'd been working on a manuscript about my life and what I'd learned and experienced as a cathartic experience, but I'd shelved it. Now I've got plenty of time on my hands and the words come tumbling out.

With any other spare moment, I start working through the books on my shelf above my makeshift desk. One catches my eye. It's called *My Orange Duffel Bag: A Journey to Radical Change*. I've had it for several months ever since a colleague introduced me to the author at a conference for police personnel. I pull it off the shelf one night when I can't sleep anyway. The guy's story is similar to mine—homelessness as a teen, abuse as a kid, never feeling like he belonged, and finding redemption through athletics and mentors. His transformation came at Georgia Tech. I found mine in the military.

Things start to feel really shaky between Denise and me. When I get back from the Christmas holidays in 2014, I get scared. Alone with my thoughts, I start to imagine what my life would be like if she decides to file for divorce. I am on the verge of panic at the thought of losing at love a third time.

I notice that the coauthor of Sam Bracken's book is based in Metro Atlanta. I find her author's page on Facebook and send her a message about my manuscript. No response.

I guess that's that. It's probably no good anyway.

A week later, I am feeling lower than I've felt in years. I decide to reach out one more time. To my shock, she responds almost immediately and agrees to read my manuscript.

I send it off the next day. She writes me back telling me that she thinks I have something to say that will help others.

I think about all that I've learned through the power of storytelling. I've been inspired by others who were willing to share their own struggles along with their triumphs.

We meet several times for interview sessions and to work on the book project.

Then another miracle happens. My commanding officer helps me to transition, and I get an offer to accept a position in the Orlando area again. I spend as much time on the weekends as I can until I get reassigned to Orlando. I return to school to requalify as an Inspector General. Once again I am honored to take on that duty, and it is a fitting terminal assignment.

I continue to work on the book project, and as I do, I find my next step in my education—probably my toughest assignment yet. I am forced through the process to examine my own heart and actions, to search my soul for anger and bitterness, to seek forgiveness and give forgiveness, and to confront who I am. Most of all, I must decide if I am willing to step up and serve others for the rest of my life.

If I hadn't been assigned to Fort Gillem, I'm not sure I would have been motivated to take the next step toward what I now know with certainty is my destiny. God moves in mysterious ways.

A NEW MISSION

It doesn't take any more energy to create a big dream than it does to create a little one.

—General Wesley Clark

As I sit on my lanai of my home in Hilo, Hawaii, I smell the heady aroma of the plumeria tree in the air. I look over a yard green from the falling rain, and I reminisce about what it took to get here, owning my own home in Hawaii. Making this night even more special is that family has joined us on this trip for my preretirement party. Several years ago, when I commanded soldiers here, we bought this house on the Big Island.

Inaugural team members Rafael Medina, Mark, and Pedro Laboy at the thirtieth reunion of the all US military taekwondo teams in 2015

Russell Mauga, a renowned singer/songwriter and musician, is playing some of the best local music I have ever heard. Earlier in the evening, he shared that he played at Dog the Bounty Hunter's wedding. That made me laugh. I figure if he's good enough for Dog, he's more than enough for this Missouri country boy.

Russell's pastor and church join the celebration and, at our request, perform a traditional Hawaiian blessing ceremony for our house.

I have so much to be thankful for. The beauty of the Pacific Ocean and the tropical forest transports me back to why I love Hawaii so much: the scuba diving, the aloha spirit, and the mountains. When I first arrived in Hawaii in 2006, a double rainbow captivated me as I drove with my first convoy on top of the mountain. The day I did my last training on the Big Island, another one glowed in the sky. My first sergeant said it was a sign.

I agree. With the rainbow, God gave us a reminder that He keeps his promises. Beauty can come out of even the worst storms.

I have learned some powerful lessons. I cannot control the actions of others. I can only work on myself. I have learned that life is not always fair. There were things I did not like about myself and things I should have never had to endure. But I've learned to be grateful and embrace who I am and to let go of anger. My character has been built from failing in my personal and professional life many times.

I have learned that when you endure failure, you can grow from it if you dust yourself off and get back up to push forward. I have learned that achievement only comes when you are willing to take a risk and give your all.

I have experienced almost every emotion known to the human condition in my life—the highest highs, to the lowest lows. I have traveled the country and have seen every state but two. I have experienced things and taken risks that most would never take. I have lost and I have won. I am a survivor, not a victim.

Only recently have I learned that achievement is only part of the equation. I spent years striving after one goal after another—dangling from the vine of one achievement before I grabbed hold of the next. I was addicted to the thrill of the chase.

In the last three years while working on this book, I've come to understand that it is connection with others that is most important.

What we have, the titles we earn, that fancy car in the driveway, or the large bank account is not what makes us successful. I have learned that it is doing what you love that makes you successful.

The things we go through define us. I had no integrity at first; I stepped out of that world and joined the Army and changed that. I had no education; I stepped out of that and changed that. I was told I would not ever be an Army officer; I stepped away from that comment and stepped up and changed that. I realized that along the way, changes were happening to me that were powerful and enable me to connect with others to help them also step out and step up.

I know now that everything that has happened in my life has culminated in giving me this new mission.

To prepare for my transition, I signed up for the Army Corporate Partners program. Initially, I was assigned a mentor who did not possess the qualifications I had hoped for. Because I had decided to write a book, I wanted someone in publishing. I have learned to ask, ask, ask for what you need. My request for a mentor better aligned with my goals was honored. I was given Lisa Sharkey, who used to be the senior producer of *Good Morning America* and is now vice president of creative development at HarperCollins.

I told her some of my story, and she said, "Mark, your story is not powerful because you had a hard life. Your story is powerful because of your warrior/fighter spirit. You never gave up." She also recommended I become a certified coach. I took Jack Canfield's *The Success Principles* ten-day transformation and ultimately became a certified Jack Canfield Success Principles Coach.

One book morphed into two books: my story, which you hold in your hands, and *Warrior's Code 001*, which includes my 7 Secrets for Resilience. I am developing curriculum around the principles in that book. I like to think of what I've learned in the course of thirty-four years as a warrior and an athlete as "Resilience with a Kick." That name honors the discipline I've learned from the practice of taekwondo and from my Army training that stresses never quitting.

I am transitioning from being *in* service to being *of* service to others. The law of attraction has taught me not to be afraid to expect to attract the people who can help and support you. You must learn to ask. I have had quite a few *yes* answers, even though I felt the fear. My limiting beliefs are melting away. I have an accountability partner, I visualize what I want to manifest in my life each morning, and I repeat my affirmations daily. I went from being a teenager with no future to a man with a plan. I have learned it is not where you are, but where you want to be that is important.

Just recently, I was in a room with three hundred people in Jack Canfield's coaching program. The group was asked to get up and for the next four minutes go around the room and hug each other. My heart started pounding, and I was the only one in the room who stepped out.

Out in the hallway, I thought about why I couldn't handle that request. My heart had been stepped on so many times, I had built a wall around it and was not about to let the energy of others invade my protected turf. I realize I have also stepped on some hearts and for that I ask for forgiveness.

The following day, I met a woman I now call Dr. D who helped me see that I had built this fortress around myself because I did not want to be hurt anymore. Within two days of working with her, the block was gone. Looking into the eyes of others and having compassion for them became easy for me. That was the missing element—that connection I had ignored for so long. Sometimes you must completely tear down something before you can start to rebuild. In my case, I had to tear down the wall around my heart. It does not mean remove healthy limits with others.

What is hard is to realize that when we do need help, we should not be afraid to ask. It is in that vulnerability that we find strength.

That's another lesson I learned from this experience. It was reinforced recently when one of the top Army noncommissioned officers shared that he also sought out help with a small room full of veterans, including me.

I take care of my mother who has multiple health problems, and there are some powerful things that have happened as a result of the daily choice I now make to give my whole heart to the people in my life. She is grateful to me, and I see it in her eyes. She thanks me for everything.

Two important things are missing in this book's earlier chapters: love and joy—the love we share for our family and friends, and the joy of having others in our life who make a difference and focusing on the good in life. If you do not have others directly in your life, it does not mean you cannot live a meaningful life. Take charge of your thinking and change your mindset. It is always easy to focus on the negative. Try being grateful for seven minutes every morning for everything you have for thirty days and see how it changes you.

Today life is full of gratitude, love, and forgiveness. I am grateful for all the mentors I have had in my life. By listening to my mentors, those early seeds were planted, and my life has changed. Without caring, smart people in my life, I know that my life would look very different from the one I've been blessed with today.

Wife, Denise, Mark, and son Adam

(photo credit: Kevin Garrett)

I completed all the military and civilian education required as a leader to become a full Colonel in the US Army, but ultimately decided to retire. Why? So I could focus on this calling: *to empower those who have dedicated their lives to serving our great country to be strong, be resilient, and stay in the fight.*

Love is the missing link. The biggest lesson I've learned is to love myself and to love others. Without that, nothing matters in the end. Remember, in vulnerability, there is strength. Lose the ego, my friends. I invite you to step out and step up to your destiny. Stay in the fight.

I have so many people to thank that listing them all could fill an entire book. So many have helped my family and me in countless ways, from church pastors, property managers, attorneys, best friends, accountability partners, family caregivers, realtors, fellow athletes, officers and noncommissioned officers, doctors, authors, wealth managers, public-relations specialists, musicians, and corporate partners. I am grateful for you all and the support you have given me while working on this life work. I am so overwhelmingly happy that I finished this project. I believe with my whole heart that it will save lives.

Denise Green—Over the course of more than two decades, you've demonstrated great patience and faith as you've witnessed how crazy passionate I am and how I push past my limits on a daily basis toward my goals. When I met you, you dealt with my transitions, my anger over minor but annoying things, and my short attention span. You gave me my space when I needed it and helped me by allowing me at times to close my office door to concentrate. You watched me fight to learn to walk again, and you have seen me sob like a baby. You have been there watching me, pushing me, and ensuring balance as you stood beside me.

I never wanted to make things harder for us; I always wanted to make them easier. Now that we are on the backside of this journey together, you are the only person who knows all the adversity I've faced. You know my faults, my dreams, my failures, and my vision.

I respect you, love you, and admire you. I owe you so much for sticking with me through all of the failures and yet never giving up on me. By far, there is no other person who deserves more of my time than you, and even when I was five thousand miles away, you stayed with me. Thank you for giving me the freedom to express myself and embrace this calling. I love you.

Cherry Roth—You were my second mom. You took care of my brother and me. Your husband, Chuck, was my first real mentor. He taught me I could be a champion. You always talked firmly and fairly with us boys and fed us, hugged us, and made us feel a part of the taekwondo family. Your faith can move mountains. You are loved, and our lives are better because of you. I thank you from the bottom of my heart for what you did for me. Your strong faith is a testament to the kind of wonderful person you are, and you were a positive influence in my life. You and all your girls are wonderful, and I am deeply grateful that our life paths crossed those many years ago.

Kevin and **Echo Garrett**—Thank you both so much for welcoming me into your lives and for giving me hope and seeing in me something I did not see in myself at first. To Kevin, for being such an inspiration and brainstorming master and stand-up guy, and to you, Echo, for your talents and persistence. You took the time to listen, understand, and become a part of my journey to create a story that matters. Kevin, your ability to see things through photography is an amazing gift that led to the cover of this book. I thank you from the bottom of my heart.

I chose you, Echo, as a coauthor because of your mission statement: *I write inspiring stories.* Through this two-year journey, your guidance in writing has transformed this jumble of words into two books. You have been my sounding board. We did hours upon hours of interviews to capture the essence of what it means to stay in the fight.

You shared your home, your heart, and your talents to bring this all about. You taught me compassion and taught me to set boundaries. Your timing could not have been better. At a time when I was not feeling very motivated about life, you took on my project. It changed my future.

You and your entire family have made me feel like I have purpose, and amazing things happen almost daily now. You are truly a jewel of a person who genuinely cares for others. You handed me the book one day *Battlefield of the Mind* by Joyce Meyers, who is from my hometown of Fenton, Missouri, and a close friend of Cherry Roth's. That book helped me with my lifelong struggle with anger.

You have a heart the size of Texas and a personality that is magnetic, wonderful, and warm. You took on this project during difficult times and persevered. I am blessed to have you as the coauthor of this book and also the second one. I am eternally grateful for your whole family and the journey of stepping out to step up and showing others to never quit.

Bart Bacolini—Bart, I met you at church in Sunnyvale, California, where you made our family feel welcome. You befriended me and we went for lunch, a Coke, or just to talk about the future and faith. You were a strong mentor who knows a thing or two due to the jobs you have held. You came to my law-school graduation party and got to hear my story in a condensed form for the first time. Thank you for inviting me to the police convention in Orlando. Without that invite, I may not have ever met my coauthor, Echo Garrett, who helped me write my books. You told me that God had a plan for me coming to that event, and it was fulfilled through meeting Sam Bracken at a Franklin Covey booth. Thank you for the security and support through phone calls and face to face.

Lisa Sharkey—When I was partnered with you in the Army Corporate Partners program, I was excited to learn of your qualifications and achievements and to have someone who was willing to share their time and attention to a new author like myself. The program met every expectation, and you have kept in contact to help me along the way, even after its conclusion. I am so blessed to have your ideas, your guidance, and the examples shared to make this project a success. You also suggested I get a certification as a speaker, and I chose Jack Canfield. After traveling to Miami to meet him, I realized the impact of me following your advice. Your assistant and you made me feel welcome, and you are a great mentor to me. I got so much out of our calls.

You're the best for volunteering your time for a veteran. You brought ideas that helped me focus on what is most important— not that I had a hard life, but that the heart of my story is having the spirit of a warrior and a fighter. For that I am eternally grateful. You also pushed me to become a coach, which is one of the best things that has ever happened to me. I learned so much about myself and about helping others, a gift I will carry forward in all that I do.

Robert Sholly—I have not met many men in my life who have had their mettle tested like you have. You are a great mentor to me, and I was so impressed with your accomplishments and the book you wrote about your experiences in Vietnam. You gave me great advice on getting into the Toastmasters. Over the last two years, you have given me small but really important ideas and suggestions. We have continually communicated, and you have given me the confidence to keep going. You are a great mentor to a junior officer, and I appreciate you. Your advice did not fall on deaf ears. You're an officer and a gentleman, sir.

Jack Canfield—Your enduring evergreen message of sound principles and taking responsibility ring in my ears now every day. I am grateful to you for teaching me that I have to be 100 percent responsible; for showing me that events in our lives are just events, and it is our responses that equal the outcome; and for helping me break through my mental challenges from my past and to learn to live life with passion. You also taught me to clean up my messes and to write things down and visualize them. Although I was already doing many of the things you share, I am now laser-focused on where I want to go and what I want.

Your success principles have opened me up to the life I have always known I could live. You have given me the other side of the equation I was missing. Before I met you, I was a man without a heart. I had put it in a strong box and would not let anyone in, including the people I really love.

We are all a work in progress. I am grateful that at the most important time in my life, you came into it and have showed me the other side of what I needed. Because of you, I have revisited who I am and the value I can bring to people. I now believe in myself first and am dedicated to removing the limiting beliefs that hold me back. I am determined to love myself for who I am, to be authentic, and not be afraid to be vulnerable. Thanks to you, I've learned to hug more and smile at the world. Thank you, Jack.

We all have a story. Thank you to everyone who I did not mention who has been part of mine. You are all loved.

63rd Regional Support Command, 105
82nd Airborne, xi, 1, 53

Achievement, 110
Adams, John Quincy, 101
Aerobics, 69
Afghanistan, xii, 96–99
AIDS, xi
All American Week, 57
American Kennel Club (AKC), 87
Angelou, Maya, 63
Anger, 10
Arkansas, 39–42
Army, xi, 41–42, 95–96, 111
    advanced individual training
    (AIT), 50
    Airborne training, 51–53
    Corporate Partners program, 111
    deferred entry, 48
    father's career, 79
    joining, 42, 43, 48
    machinist, 42
    medical exam, 51
    National Guard, 80
    Reserves, xii, 87, 98
    retirement, 113
    and sports, 61
Arrest warrant, 43
Arson, 13
Atlanta, xii, xiii, 106–108
Attitude, 93
Augsburg University, 93

Babler State Park, 30
Bannister, Roger, 73
Baptism, 60, 91, 103
Baseball, 8, 28
Belt, stepfather's, 13, 14
Birthday, 8
Black Hats, 51–53
Blackhawks, 97
Blacktop work, 38–39
Book project, 108, 111
Boy Scouts, 104
Bracken, Sam, 108
Brady Bunch, The, 10

Bricks, breaking, 66
Busch Gardens, 34

C-130 aircraft, 99
Callahan Boxing Gym, 2–6, 63
Camp Ripley, 80
Canfield, Jack, 111, 112
Canoeing trip, 83–85
Car chase, 33–34
Children, 76, 77, 88, 89
Child support, 77
Chinooks, 97
Christian Taekwondo University, 59
Church, 86, 103
Churchill, Winston, 97
Clark, Wesley, 109
Class, 38, 81, 82
Clydesdales, 34
Coat, 49
College, 78
Colonel title, 113
Combat, 10
Command and General Staff College,
98, 102
    Triathlon, 104
Compassion, 84, 112
Concordia University, 95
Confidence, 57
Connection with others, 111
Construction accident, 25

D, Dr., 112
Dairy Queen, 85
De la Bruyere, Jean, 87
Department of Defense, 65
Department of the Army's Sports
Office, 64
Deployment, 97–99
Depression, 78
Deshimaru, Taisen, 1
Destiny, 114
Destiny as a soldier, 79
Determination, 78
Divorce, 76, 88
    parents', 9

Dog the Bounty Hunter, 109–110
Douglas, Buster, 63
Douglass, Frederick, 93
Drinking, 26, 71, 88
    and father, 8–9
Drum manufacturing job, 41

Ed's Attic, 80
Education, 79, 93, 106, 108, 111, 113
Ego, 114
Einstein, 107
El Paso, Texas, 28
Embryos, 90
Empowerment, 113–114
Environmental Protection Agency, 34
E-4 specialist, 80
Eureka High School, 29–30, 35
    wrestling, 30

Failure, 110
Father, xi, 8–9, 57–58, 88, 107
    visit with, 27–28
Fenton, Missouri, **7,** 9
Ferguson
    Bobby, 13
    Gary, 13, 30
    Richie, 13
Ferguson, Robert, 13–16, 29–31
    beatings, 13, 14
    at grandparents' house, 17
    separation, 16
Flood support management, 94–95
Florida, 101
Flowers, Robert, 69–70, 75
Foreign Jump Wing, 72
Fort
    Benning, 51
    Bragg, 1–6, 53, 57
    Dix, 49–53, 60, 101, 103
    Gillem, 106, 108
    Leonard Wood, 93
    Snelling, 95
Foster home, 29
France, 71–72
Frankl, Victor, 45
French Army exchange program, 71

Garbage truck job, 41

Garrett, Echo, xiii
Georgia Tech, 107
GI Bill, 78
Good Morning America, 111
Graduation, 35
Grandparents, 16–18
Gratitude, 113
Green
    Adam, xii, 91, 98, 101, 103, 104,
        105, **109, 113**
    Audrey, **26**
    Dale, 19–22, **26,** 34, 87–88, 105–
        106
    Denise, xii, 81–82, 83–86, 89–91,
        93–94, 95, 97, 98, 101, 102, 103,
        104, 106, 107–108, **113**
    Julian, 83
    Kelly, **26,** 32, **79**
    Kristie, **26**
    Mark, **26, 62, 70, 79,** 111, **113**
    Nikki, Sue Hendren, 8–10, **9,** 13–
        18, 22, 23–24, 25, **26,** 27–28, 29,
        31–32, 105–107, 113
    Stephanie, 54
Green, Jennie, 40–41, 54
    divorce, 54
Green, Kayle, 20, **26**
    murder, 88–89
Gypsies, 39–40

Harris, Bruce, 64
Hawaii, 95–96, 109–110
Helicopter, 69
Help, asking for, 112
Hendricks, Miss, 11
Hercules, 87–88
High Ridge, Jefferson County, 18
Hill, Napoleon, xi, 105
Hillsboro, Missouri, 21
Hilo, Hawaii, 109
Hip
    injury, 99, 101
    replacement, 101–102
    replacement recovery, 102–104
Hitchhiking, 29, 32
Hobo Hotel, xii
Hoosiers, fight with, 37–38
House purchase, 85–86
House Springs, Missouri, 29

Ice pond accident, 24–25
Inspector General job, 96, 97, 108
Integrity, 111
In vitro fertilization (IVF), 89
Ivory soap, 17

Jack Canfield Success Principles
Coach, 111
Jeep, 73
Jefferson City, 29
Jefferson College, 21
Jell-O, 16
Joy, 113

Kandahar, 98
Karate, 2, 19–22
Keg party, 23
Kent, Jesse, **17**
Kmart, 23
Kool-Aid, 16
Korean Taekwondo Association of
American, 59

Laboy, Pedro, 1–6, 58, 61–62, 63, 64,
109
Lakeland, Florida, 40
Law of attraction, 112
Law school, 97, 98
    graduation, 105
Levis, 33
Lieutenant Colonel, 98
    promotion, 105
Lifelong learner, 95
Lincoln, Abraham, 49
Love, 113, 114
Luck, Jim, 24–25
Luck family, 24–25, 29
    fireworks stand, 24
Lynn, Loretta, 10

Machinist job, 75
Marijuana, 29
Marriage, 40–41, 74, 86
Master's degree, 95
Mauga, Russell, 109–110

Mayes, Master Myong, 5
Mayo Clinic, 89
Medina, Rafael, 1–6, 61–62, 64, **109,**
Mentors, 65, 111
Meramec River Bridge fight, 32
Minnesota Military Academy Officer
Candidate School, 80–82, 83–86
    graduation, 82
Moberly, Missouri, 7, 16
Mohawk, xii
Moral, Welfare, and Recreation
program, 62, 63
Mother. *See* Green, Nikki, Sue
Hendren
Moving, 93, 95
Murder of brother, 88–89
*My Orange Duffel Bag: A Journey to
Radical Change* (Bracken), xiii, 107
Myrtle Beach, South Carolina, 73

Namibia, Africa, 93
National championship (1985), **67**
National Guard, xi, 8, 34, 77–78
Navy, 87
New York Life, 8
North Carolina Taekwondo State
Championship, **5**
Northwest High School, 29

Officer Candidate School (OCS), 80,
82
Officer commission, 93
Oledan, Leo, 64
Olympic team, 34
Operation, 17
Orlando, xii, 106–108

Pacific Ocean, 110
Pagnol, Marcel, 23
Parachutes, 54, 57
Peoria, Illinois, 22
Picket run, 70
Plasma, 40
Post-traumatic stress, xiii
Pregnancy, 41, 74, 75, 90
Pride, 82
Probation, 43

Rainbow, 110
Rape and attempted murder, family member, 88
Readjustment after war zone, 103–104
Real estate broker job, 75–77
Red Cross, 94
Reenlistment, 75
Reserve Officers' Training Corps, 82
Resilience, 111–112
Riden, Dwayne, 50
Rochester, Minnesota, 86
Rochester Community College, 80
Roth, Charles, 18–22
Rottweiler, 87

School, problems in, 11, 26, 35
Second Lieutenant, 94
Sell, Brenda, 59
Sell, Senior Grand Master Edward, 3, 58–60, 65–67
    rules, 59
Senior Skip Day, 34–35, 88
Sharkey, Lisa, 111
Siblings, 8–9, 19–22, **26,** 34, 87–88, 105–106
Skype, 97, 98
Soldier
    of the Month, 70
    of the Year, 70
Sorry!, 17
St. Louis
    Cardinals, 8
    County, 31
    County jail abuse, 45–47
St. Mary's Hospital, 91
Strength, 55, 112, 114
Stress, 78
Success Principles, The (Canfield), 111

Suicide of stepfather, 106
Summer, childhood, 7–8
Survivor, 110

Tac Sergeants. *See* Black Hats
Taekwondo, 1–6, 18–22, 58, 61–87
    black belt, 34
    brown belt, 32
Tampa, 106
Teamsters, 14
Temper, 11
Times Beach, 34
    police, 48
Tire jack, 32
Top Gun, 73
Tournament, first, 21
Trailer, mother's, 18
Trophies, 22

United States Taekwondo Union (USTU) Championship, 64
United Van Lines, 10
US Army taekwondo team, **62**
    shirts, 63
US military taekwondo reunion, 109

Vulnerability, 112, 114

Warren, Rick, 37
Warrior's Code 001 (Drew), xiv, 111
Washington, Booker T., 7
Weight loss, 101
Western Union, 40
West Point, 82
William Taft Law School, 105
Winning, 65
Wintle, Walter D., 27
World Taekwondo Championship, 59

Mark E. Green started as a private in the US Army in December 1982 and retired as a Lieutenant Colonel on October 1, 2017, without a break in service. He gave twenty-four years of active duty, including three years in the 82nd Airborne, served in the National Guard as a combat arms–enlisted soldier and officer, and served as an Army Reserve full-time soldier. He served in Afghanistan as an Inspector General in charge of the

southern half of the country, along the red desert from the borders of Pakistan to Iran. As a young soldier, he was also a pioneer black-belt member of the first ever taekwondo team that went to the US Nationals and that led to the future All Army teams who became part of the Army World Class Athlete Program. That first pioneer team and all subsequent teams have competed annually for spots on the US Olympic team.

Green has devoted the remainder of his career to helping those in military service, veterans, and their families with resiliency and transition. He holds a doctorate of law from Taft Law School, Santa Ana, California, and a master's degree in organizational management and communications from Concordia University, St. Paul, Minnesota. He is also a Jack Canfield–Certified Success Principles Coach, and a graduate of Boots to Business program of Syracuse University and of the Army Corporate Partner (ACP) Mentorship Program. He completed Dynamic Speakers International SCORRE and is a member and officer of Lake Nona Toastmasters. He volunteers his time as a mentor for the Camaraderie Foundation that supports veterans in transition.

His purpose in sharing his story in *Step Out, Step Up: Lessons Learned from a Lifetime of Transition and Military Service* is to encourage others to have hope and recognize that no matter where you come from, you can achieve your dreams. In *Warrior's Code 001*, he shares his secrets to developing a mindset that boosts resiliency and smooths transitions. He developed these strategies from his own experiences with his family, hard-earned lessons, and education, and is developing a curriculum around them.

His company, My Silver Boots, LLC, is a Florida-based, veteran-owned, made-in-the-USA small business, which has earmarked 10 percent of its profits to be divided among the following nonprofits that serve veterans and their families; underserved youth dealing with poverty, homelessness, or foster care; and US Army athletes.

Green resides with wife, Denise, teenage son Adam, and his mom in Florida. As one of the nation's top experts on military transition, Green thrives on speaking about resilience and transformational change.

To book Mark E. Green for a keynote or to teach a workshop, please contact him through his website.

http://www.mark.green

Echo Montgomery Garrett is the coauthor of *My Orange Duffel Bag: A Journey to Radical Change*, winner of the American Society of Journalists and Authors (ASJA) 2013 Arlene Eisenberg Award for Writing that Makes a Difference, which is only awarded every three years to a book that's made the biggest difference in people's lives. The book won six other national awards in the categories of self-help and young  adult nonfiction. It also won two international awards for best book design, and it garnered Garrett the title of Georgia Author of the Year from the Georgia chapter of the National League of American Pen Women. She cofounded the Orange Duffel Bag Initiative (www.theodbi.org), an award-winning nonprofit that does life-plan coaching based on the principles in the book for homeless youth, high-poverty youth, and those aging out of foster care. She has written or contributed to fourteen other books, including award-winner *Why Don't They Just Get a Job?: One Couple's Mission to End Poverty in Their Community*. The Marietta, Georgia–based writer's work has been published in more than one hundred national media outlets, including *Parade, Delta Sky, Success,* and the *Atlanta-Journal Constitution*. She has been interviewed on *Good Morning America,* CNBC, CNN, and NY-1, and has served as editor in chief of *Atlanta Woman* magazine. Married to professional photographer Kevin Garrett, the couple resides in Marietta, Georgia. Their son Connor is the CEO of StudyHubb.com, and son Caleb is a professional fly-fishing guide in Missoula, Montana.